Toys to Tools

Connecting Student Cell Phones to Education

Liz Kolb

International Society for Technology in Education
EUGENE, OREGON ▪ WASHINGTON, DC

Toys to Tools
Connecting Student Cell Phones to Education

Liz Kolb

Publications Director: *Courtney Burkholder*
Acquisitions Editor: *Jeff V. Bolkan*
Production Editors: *Lynda Gansel, Lanier Brandau*
Production Coordinator: *Rachel Bannister*
Graphic Designer, Book and Cover Design: *Signe Landin*

Copy Editor: *Lynne Ertle*
Indexer: *Seth Maislin, Potomac Indexing*
Book Production: *Tracy Cozzens*

Library of Congress Cataloging-in-Publication Data

Kolb, Liz.
Toys to tools : connecting student cell phones to education / Liz Kolb.
   p. cm.
  Includes bibliographical references and index.
  ISBN 978-1-56484-247-3 (pbk.)
   1. Educational technology. 2. Cellular telephones. 3. Education—Effect of technological innovations on. 4. Mobile communication systems—United States.   I. Title.
  LB1028.3.K65 2008
  371.33—dc22

                                       2008036554

First Edition
ISBN: 978-1-56484-247-3
Printed in the United States of America

International Society for Technology in Education (ISTE)
Washington, DC, Office:
  1710 Rhode Island Ave. NW, Suite 900, Washington, DC 20036-3132
Eugene, Oregon, Office:
  180 West 8th Ave., Suite 300, Eugene, OR 97401-2916
Order Desk: 1.800.336.5191
Order Fax: 1.541.302.3778
Customer Service: orders@iste.org
Book Publishing: books@iste.org
Rights and Permissions: permissions@iste.org
Web: www.iste.org

About ISTE

The International Society for Technology in Education (ISTE) is the trusted source for professional development, knowledge generation, advocacy, and leadership for innovation. A nonprofit membership association, ISTE provides leadership and service to improve teaching, learning, and school leadership by advancing the effective use of technology in PK–12 and teacher education.

Home of the National Educational Technology Standards (NETS), the Center for Applied Research in Educational Technology (CARET), and the National Educational Computing Conference (NECC), ISTE represents more than 85,000 professionals worldwide. We support our members with information, networking opportunities, and guidance as they face the challenge of transforming education. To find out more about these and other ISTE initiatives, visit our Web site at www. iste.org.

As part of our mission, ISTE Book Publishing works with experienced educators to develop and produce practical resources for classroom teachers, teacher educators, and technology leaders. Every manuscript we select for publication is carefully peer-reviewed and professionally edited. We look for content that emphasizes the effective use of technology where it can make a difference—increasing the productivity of teachers and administrators; helping students with unique learning styles, abilities, or backgrounds; collecting and using data for decision making at the school and district levels; and creating dynamic, project-based learning environments that engage 21st-century learners. We value your feedback on this book and other ISTE products. E-mail us at books@iste.org.

Lesson Plans...39

   Lesson Plan 1 ▪ Oral History Project...........................40

   Lesson Plan 2 ▪ Poetry Slam Podcast.........................49

   Lesson Plan 3 ▪ Oral Quiz.......................................54

   Lesson Plan 4 ▪ Virtual Science Symposium......................63

   Lesson Plan 5 ▪ Physics Sound Waves...........................67

Chapter 4

Cell Phones as Cameras and Camcorders 71

Cell Phones as Cameras..72

Cell Phones as Camcorders...75

Classroom Use of Cell Phones as Cameras and Camcorders............77

Lesson Plans...82

   Lesson Plan 6 ▪ Local Landmarks Photoblog....................83

   Lesson Plan 7 ▪ Geometry Digital Storybook....................86

   Lesson Plan 8 ▪ Rock Identification...........................91

   Lesson Plan 9 ▪ PhotoMapping.................................94

   Lesson Plan 10 ▪ Geo-Insects.................................98

   Lesson Plan 11 ▪ Telenovela................................. 103

   Lesson Plan 12 ▪ Scavenger Hunt............................. 108

Chapter 5

Developing Classroom Projects for Cell Phones 111

Ringtones.. 112

Wallpaper and Logos... 113

Text Messaging.. 114

Mobile Web Sites.. 118

Mobile Blogs.. 118

Mobile Surveys and Polls.. 119

Mobile Presentations and Enhanced Podcasts............................ 120

Classroom Ideas... 121

Parental Involvement.. 126

Lesson Plans 126

Lesson Plan 13 ▪ Math Ringtone Raps or Jingles 127

Lesson Plan 14 ▪ Travel Postcards 131

Lesson Plan 15 ▪ Who Am I? 134

Lesson Plan 16 ▪ Inquiry Question Icebreaker 137

Lesson Plan 17 ▪ Think-Alouds 140

Lesson Plan 18 ▪ Science Activism Project 145

Lesson Plan 19 ▪ Stay Healthy! 148

Lesson Plan 20 ▪ Mobile Homework Help Blog 151

Lesson Plan 21 ▪ Scientific Survey 154

Lesson Plan 22 ▪ Revolutionary War Enhanced Podcast 158

Lesson Plan 23 ▪ Elections 164

Chapter 6

Cell Phones as Research and Organizational Tools 169

The Benefits of Web Surfing by Cell Phone 170

Web Site Access 171

Classroom Web Sites and Educational Resources 171

Libraries with Text-Messaging Services 172

Calendars, Voice Recorders, and Notepads 173

Calculators 174

Chapter 7

Cell Phones as Management Tools 175

Student Supervision 176

Group Activities 176

Field Trips and Extracurricular Events 177

Student Safety 178

Mobile Citizen Journalism 179

Student Absenteeism 180

Teacher Absenteeism 180

Struggling Students 181

Connecting with Parents 182

Homework Help 182

Chapter 8

Cell Phones in Preschool and Lower Elementary Learning 185

Etiquette Starts Early 186
Student Ownership.. 189
One Cell Phone Outside the Classroom 189
One Cell Phone Inside the Classroom 190

Chapter 9

The Future of Cell Phones in Schools 191

Educational Software.. 192
Writing, Literature, and Textbooks................................ 192
MP3 Players, Recorders, and Radios............................... 193
Live Streaming, Audio Editing, and Video Editing 194
GPS Tools and Tracking.. 195
Digital Projectors.. 195
Faxes and Scanners... 196
Mobile Storage... 196
E-Commerce.. 197
Point and Click 198
Assistive Technology 198
Starter Phones and Phone Plans 199
M-Government 199
Solar-Powered Cell Phones... 200

Chapter 10

More Web 2.0 Resources for Cell Phones.................... 201

Podcasting 202
Voice Mail 203
Conferencing 203
Mobile Notes 204
Mobile Web Sites... 205
RSS, E-mail, and Favorites... 205
Camera and Camcorder Resources................................. 206
Reference and Organizational Tools................................ 206
Logos, Wallpaper, and Ringtones.................................. 207

Text Messaging 208
Mobile Shopping 208
Mobile Quizzes 208
Music and Art 209
Health Education 210

References 211

**National Educational Technology Standards
for Students (NETS•S)** 216

Index 219

Credits 230

phones belong on a school campus at all (Project Tomorrow, 2006b). Instead of spending time, energy, and money creating policies to fight cell phone use in schools, educators could spend their time finding useful ways to integrate these devices as knowledge construction, data collection, and collaborative communication tools to help students become more competitive in the digital world. I have observed the controversy and decided to gather and present the resources I have found that provide examples for utilizing cell phones as classroom learning tools in hopes that other educators might find these resources useful and worth exploring.

This book is for K–12 classroom teachers and technology integration specialists who are interested in using cell phones as learning tools inside or outside of the classroom. Although readers should be familiar with various technologies, such as podcasting and blogging, they need not be experts. I have included step-by-step tutorials for using many of the resources described in this book.

As a former technology coordinator, I am well aware of the financial straits facing most schools; therefore, many of the Web resources I discuss in this book are inexpensive or free. I am also sensitive to educational policies that bar cell phones from schools; therefore, I describe cell phone learning activities that can be conducted outside of school. Most of the activities and lessons described in this book, in fact, allow for cell phone use only outside of school, such as on a field trip or for homework, and the work can be built on inside the classroom (without students needing to bring the cell phones onto school grounds). Because the majority of students who have cell phones are over the age of 12, this book emphasizes learning activities at the secondary level (Grades 6–12). However, there is good reason to consider how cell phones could be learning tools for younger students. Consequently, chapter 8 describes how PK–5 teachers could benefit from including cell phones in learning.

Recognizing that every educator has a different comfort level with technology, the learning activities I describe range from the intuitive (cell phone basics) to the more complex (downloading and editing cell phone audio or photo files to use with video-editing software). I also introduce ideas on how cell phones may be useful in helping teachers with their classroom and student management. This book also considers several issues involved with integrating cell phones into classroom learning, such as security, access, and finance. I address those concerns by providing potential solutions. Ultimately, the goal of this book is to encourage educators to introduce cell phones to students as potential learning tools and lifelong professional tools, rather than viewing them solely as a social toy.

Chapter 1

Cell Phones as Learning Tools

This chapter focuses on the potential benefits of using cell phones in learning. Although the media often emphasize the reasons why educators do not or should not consider cell phones as learning tools, it is important to contemplate the other side of the argument—why educators should consider cell phones as learning tools. This chapter briefly describes the research in literacy education, learning technologies, and youth studies that supports integrating cell phones into schools. At the same time, it is still important to explore the common concerns that educators have with integrating cell phones into their classrooms, and chapter 2 explores the many reasons why cell phones are controversial for classroom instruction.

Bringing Student Culture into the Classroom

Researchers who have studied the disconnect between the culture of student home life and student experiences in school believe that if the home culture of students is integrated into their classroom learning, they are more likely to be academically successful (Cazden & Leggett, 1981; Jordan, 1985; Mohatt & Erikson, 1981). Experts in the field of literacy over the last decade focused on broadening the definition of literacy by studying student culture outside of school as a resource for adolescent literacy learning (Alvermann & Xu, 2003; Bean, Bean, & Bean, 1999; Chandler-Olcott & Mahar, 2003; Finders, 1996; Moje, 2002).

Today, technology is often a large part of the literacy practices of our youth outside of school and is considered one of the multiple literacies in today's society. Many researchers believe that multiple literacies provide a bridge between the real-life texts of the community and school learning. In addition, using a multiple literacy approach to classroom instruction enables students to understand, use, and critically evaluate the multimodal texts of the 21st century.

According to Elizabeth Moje (2000), in "'To Be Part of the Story': The Literacy Practices of Gangsta Adolescents":

> We can become more aware of what adolescents can do and of the power and sophistication of those practices that are so often dismissed as vandalism or laziness. If we reconceptualize our literacy theory, research, and pedagogy to acknowledge the tools at use for making meaning in unsanctioned practices, to work with the strengths that our students already possess, and to teach students how to navigate the many discursive spaces called for in new and complex times … then we may be able to teach students tools that provide them with opportunities to be part of and to construct multiple stories in many different social worlds. (p. 685)

The issues of youth literacy and everyday technology that Moje pinpoints are common concerns. Educators dismiss cell phones, instant messaging, and other popular technology communication tools as "distracting" to classroom learning. Yet if educational technology theory, research, and pedagogy are reconceptualized to include the tools and knowledge that students already possess, then students will have better opportunities to connect learning inside and outside of school.

Digital technology literacy is a form of cultural capital. Moje and Sutherland (2003) argue that students need to learn the tools and practices that have cultural capital in different communities, and how to effectively navigate those tools. Chandler-Olcott and Mahar (2003) assert that classrooms that integrate technology-mediated literacy practices within everyday social learning communities have the potential to promote more academically related interests within the school than classrooms lacking such integration. Bruce (1997) goes further to suggest that we must embrace and acknowledge new technologies, rather than ignore or fear the new literacies that are part of these innovations. Often the literacy practices in today's communities and in traditional classrooms are radically different. For students to be successful in the future they must learn how to use different literacy tools in various knowledge-building communities.

Connecting Everyday Digital Culture with Classroom Learning

Although many classroom teachers use software created for educational purposes, teachers seem to draw the line at everyday technologies used by youth outside the classroom. This disconnect between how students communicate outside of school and how they learn and communicate inside the classroom is growing (Levin, Arafeh, Lenhart, & Rainie, 2002; Tell, 2000). Outside of school, students communicate through instant messaging, online chatting, cell phones, e-mail, BlackBerry devices, Web cams, video games, digital media players, and other network and digital technologies. The Kaiser Family Foundation (2005) named today's youth the M-generation because of the adolescents' ability to multitask with a variety of media devices at one time, such as talking on the cell phone, instant messaging, and writing an essay all at once. Yet teachers assume students are the same as they have always been, and the traditional methods that worked for teachers when they were students will work for students today (Prensky, 2001).

Students are aware of and sensitive to their teachers' dislike of their social "toys." Teachers have very little appreciation for these new devices and the communication and knowledge-building skills students have developed as a result of them (Levin et al., 2002). Instructors repeatedly let students know their everyday social toys are not acceptable in the learning environment. Some teachers see the technologies of youth as distracting, time consuming, wasteful, and even harmful. One of the most popular youth technologies is the cell phone. This technology, however, is not

"toys," educators need to bring those "toys" into educational activities so students can learn to use them as tools of knowledge. The issue is not whether educators should use the media tools of the M-generation in the classroom; rather, the issue is how to help teachers learn to utilize the media tools effectively for knowledge construction.

Digital Etiquette

Another reason to consider introducing cell phones in learning is to promote digital etiquette, a concept foreign to most people. According to a recent study by the Pew Internet & American Life Project, "How Americans Use Their Cell Phones":

> More than a quarter of cell phone owners (28%) admit they sometimes do not drive as safely as they should while they use their mobile devices.... Furthermore, 82% of all Americans and 86% of cell users report being irritated at least occasionally by loud and annoying cell users who conduct their calls in public places. Indeed, nearly one in ten cell phone owners (8%) admit they themselves have drawn criticism or irritated stares from others when they are using their cell phones in public. (Rainie & Keetyer, 2006, p. 1)

An educator's job is to help students navigate and stay safe in their media world. Students are often unaware of and indifferent to the consequences of their use and misuse of technology (Rainie, 2006). Currently, many students do not worry about protecting their own privacy or the privacy of others when using digital media. For example, 55% of students do not care whether the digital material they use is copyrighted (Rainie, 2006). Additionally, only 25% of students consider online safety and cost a concern when using the Internet (Project Tomorrow, 2006a). When it comes to etiquette, students ages 10–17 often do not seem to understand appropriate cell phone use. According to the Disney Mobile Survey (2007), while nine out of ten 10- to 17-year-olds believe they are polite on their cell phones, 52% admit to sending text messages at the movie theater, while 28% admit to sending text messages at the dinner table. These statistics demonstrate that teens and tweens are unaware of cell phone etiquette, and educators have an opportunity to teach them appropriate uses of this communication device.

Instead of spending time, energy, and money creating policies to fight cell phone use in schools, we are better served by directing our resources toward finding useful ways to integrate these devices as knowledge construction, data collection, and collaborative communication tools, and toward teaching digital etiquette. Parents may appreciate the help. Rosen (2006) found that only one-third of parents have seen their children's MySpace page and only 16% of them check it on a regular basis. Although this does not relate directly to cell phones, it demonstrates that parents may need some assistance in monitoring their children and teaching them about digital etiquette.

Bottom-Up Approach to Technology in Schools

Historically, access to educational hardware and software in classrooms has not guaranteed that teachers will use the tools in an effective way (Cuban, 1986; Cuban, Kirkpatrick, & Peck, 2001). During the last 10 years, K–12 schools and state and federal governments have spent around $6.9 billion on computer hardware, Internet access, wiring, software, servers, and other digital equipment to make today's technology available to students and teachers (Kleiman, 2000). Despite all the effort to give teachers and students access to technology, Cuban et al. (2001) found that access to educational software and hardware did not lead to its widespread use in classroom learning. The most creative and frequent uses of technology have not been linked to curricula (Becker, 2000). In addition, Becker (2000) argues that the most creative uses of computer technology were found in stand-alone computer classes rather than the mainstream core courses.

If there is so much access to technology in schools, why is it underused? Why aren't students more motivated to learn with the technology available in today's schools? Cuban (1986) argues one reason that technology integration has historically failed in schools is because the technology is initiated with a top-down approach, in which the administrators force certain technologies onto teachers, and teachers in turn force certain technologies onto students. In effect, educators are increasing the barrier between the technology tools students use in their everyday lives and the technology tools they interact with in school. Students want to use cell phone technology, and research has found that 97% of students would like a relaxation of the rules of cell phones in schools (Project Tomorrow, 2006a). Integrating cell phones constitutes a bottom-up approach to technology in the classroom, in which the students (not the teachers) are the community of learners who are "proposing" the technologies used in the classroom. Soloway, Guzdial, and Hay (1994) call for more contextualized technologies in the classroom. Although they emphasize designing learner-centered software for the classroom, we rarely see widespread use of software designed for educational purposes.

Instead of designing new software, let's use the everyday software and hardware students already own (or are free to own or use) and are already motivated to interact with, such as their cell phones. By doing so, we may be able to create better learning opportunities and resources for our students that can easily extend beyond the classroom walls.

Although it is easy to theorize that cell phones may be a way to connect classroom learning with everyday youth culture, it is quite another to illustrate how cell phones can become instructional tools. The following chapters provide many examples of how cell phones can be used outside the classroom as a learning tool that connects to activities inside the classroom. In addition, I highlight cutting-edge teachers who have begun to tap in to the concept of using cell phones in learning. Also included are step-by-step tutorials of many Web 2.0 resources.

Chapter 2

Concerns with Cell Phones in the Classroom

Using cell phones for classroom learning raises legitimate concerns. Although there are currently no federal or state laws that prohibit using cell phones in the classroom or for learning, many schools have policies against even bringing cell phones to school. As a result, teachers often assume they cannot and should not consider the cell phone as a learning tool. As mentioned earlier, this book emphasizes learning activities using cell phones outside the classroom, therefore not violating any school rules against cell phones in the classroom. However, there are many other concerns besides bringing cell phones to class that educators and parents have with cell phones in learning.

This chapter discusses these many concerns of using cell phones as classroom learning tools: teachers having control over cell phones in the classroom, cell phone etiquette, student access to cell phones, the costs associated with cell phone use, advertising on cell phone–compatible Web 2.0 Web sites, students publishing from their cell phone to the Internet, and school security when cell phones are allowed to be used in the building. Although there is not one easy solution to these concerns, some potential solutions to all of these concerns are provided. It is important for teachers, administrators, and the community to decide if and how they would like to include cell phones as learning tools, but it is also important they make an informed decision based on more than media hype or an assumption that cell phones are purely the social toys of a younger generation. The topics presented in this chapter allow for an open discussion of both the concerns and the potential benefits of using cell phones as learning tools inside and outside of school.

Cell Phones in School

As mentioned earlier, many school districts have strong policies prohibiting students from bringing their cell phones into the school building. Because these policies may be difficult to change, cell phones do not have to be brought to school in order to be used for the learning activities in this book. Field trips and homework assignments are two ways that students can take advantage of their cell phones as learning tools without having to bring them to the classroom.

Students can take pictures, capture video, or record audio outside of school and post their data before coming to class to any of a number of Web 2.0 sites, such as Gcast, Gabcast, Hipcast, Blogger, Flickr, Photobucket, or Eyespot (these resources and associated cell phone activities will be discussed in upcoming chapters). The next day in class students can log on to their sites and download the data for class projects. They can also take advantage of the online editing and posting tools on Web 2.0 sites to further develop movies, create slideshows, design blogs, or perform other activities with their audio and image recordings without having a cell phone in the classroom. This way the students are learning how to use their social toy as a data collection tool and the school policy has not been violated. Once students are successful with using cell phones outside of school as a learning tool, teachers could approach their administrators about changing policy to allow cell phones in school for content-related learning opportunities.

Classroom Control

Although keeping students on task without cell phones in the classroom is hard enough, many teachers worry it will become increasingly difficult when students have cell phones at their desk. Teachers worry that the cell phone is simply another toy to distract students from the lesson. In addition, one major argument against allowing cell phones in the classroom is that camera and camcorder phones can be used to take inappropriate pictures, which can then be published to the Internet, unbeknownst to the teacher or the subject of the pictures. Although the easy solution is to stick with cell phone activities that occur outside the classroom, I'd like to propose solutions that allow constructive cell phone use inside the classroom.

One solution is for teachers to simply take control. Teachers can control when students bring in their cell phones and where they keep them during class (such as collecting them as the students enter the classroom and holding them until it is time to use them). Also, remember that any tool can be distracting and even harmful if used inappropriately in the classroom (students still pass notes and doodle on paper when they should be paying attention in class). The key is to structure and control when the cell phones are used and when they are not used.

Another solution is to set up a social contract with students before engaging in any cell phone activities. A social contract is an agreement between the teacher and students about how, when, why, and where cell phones will be used in the classroom. In the social contract you can set up regulations as well as consequences for not obeying the contract. For example, you could require that students leave their cell phones off in the front of the room until it is time to use them for the project. The consequence for noncompliance could be missing out on the cell phone project and doing an alternative assignment instead. Often when social contracts are set up with student input, they are more likely to "stick to their contract." In addition, it is important to provide parents with permission forms that state the nature of the activity and include the social contract. Through the permission forms you can let students and parents know that using cell phones in the classroom is a privilege and that there are consequences for violating the privilege.

Cell Phone Etiquette

Many educators worry about using cell phones as educational tools because they think that students misuse them as social toys. We often get annoyed when we are sitting in a library and a student is talking loudly on a cell phone or we are in a movie theater and a child nearby is text messaging during the entire film. As irritated as we get, we don't take the time to talk with the person about why we are annoyed and why certain uses of a cell phone can be inappropriate. Since cell phones are becoming ubiquitous in our society, it is important to talk with students about cell phone etiquette inside and outside of school. Students consider their cell phones a fashion accessory (Selian & Srivastava, 2004). Our students need to understand when it is appropriate and when it is not appropriate to use cell phones. Students need to understand how text messaging and digital jargon (such as LOL) may not always be acceptable for their future professional lives. In addition, they should understand some simple etiquette of when to turn off cell phones and when not to answer the phone (it is shocking how many students will answer their cell phone in the middle of an important meeting).

Student Access

Educators often worry that because some students do not have their own cell phone (especially at the elementary level or in lower income areas), it may not be fair to have assignments that require a cell phone. Although not every student may have a cell phone, that is not necessarily a reason to exclude cell phones as learning tools. There is a very good chance that the students who do not have a cell phone eventually will have one, and will consider it an essential communication device in the near future. By not teaching these students how a cell phone can be a learning tool, they may never be educated on how this "toy" has the ability to help them professionally in their future.

Don't count yourself out if not all your students have cell phones. Many activities in this book require only one cell phone for the entire class. As a matter of fact, if only the teacher has a cell phone, students can still use it to do activities. For example, an entire radio broadcast can be created with one cell phone, with students taking turns doing their individual broadcasts. A virtual conference can be done with the entire class and one cell phone. In elementary school, the cell phone can be used for a "center" activity (see chapter 8 for more about center activities and cell phones). If asking students to use cell phones for their homework assignment, the teacher can allow students without cell phones to use a landline to call Gabcast or Gcast (which have toll-free numbers), so that no cell phone is necessary to complete the assignment. Teachers can also put students in groups so at least one group member has access to a cell phone. For picture and video assignments, students without a cell phone can upload images and videos taken with regular digital cameras or camcorders. Just as many educators get by and are often very creative with only one computer in the classroom, they can also get by with only one cell phone in the classroom.

Financial Considerations

The financial angle is one of the most important factors to consider when using cell phones and Web 2.0 sites. Although most of the Web 2.0 sites are free to use, minor fees may be added to your students' (or their parents') cell phone bill. Gabcast, YouMail, and Gcast phone numbers are toll free, and as long as students stay within their calling minutes per month, there is no extra cell phone charge for using these audio-recoding sites. Although the online resources for photo, ringtone, wallpaper, and video storage are often free, the cell phone text message to "text" your photo, ringtone, or video to your online account may not be free. The cell phone provider may charge the student or teacher, depending on the individual cell phone plan.

This is a good time to talk with your students about being knowledgeable about their cell phone plans, and to help them realize that cell phone text messaging or calls are not always free, and they should be responsible cell phone users. This creates an opportunity for students to learn about their cell phone plan and avoid unnecessarily large bills associated with text messaging or Web surfing. Parents may also appreciate this! Another option can be writing a mini-grant for a classroom or school set of cell phones with a basic text messaging and calling plan. Some cell phone companies may be interested in teaming with schools to develop curriculum and activities in exchange for free or very inexpensive cell phones. Schools are often writing mini-grants for other PDA devices such as Palm Pilots, so why not cell phones? In addition, with a classroom set, the teacher can control when and how the cell phones are used.

Advertising

Although Web 2.0 is fast becoming a free and easy alternative to purchasing expensive software, some Web 2.0 sites for use with cell phones have advertisements. It is understandable that educators worry about the advertisements students are exposed to when surfing the Web. Although no inappropriate advertising was witnessed while researching this book, that does not mean students will never come across something inappropriate while using the sites mentioned in this book. At the same time, it is not in our students' best interest to disallow them to use Web 2.0 sites or keep them from experiencing the many engaging learning activities mentioned in this book simply because of the advertising they might come across. As a matter of fact, in this day and age, it is vital that we talk with students about the power of advertising on the Internet and what to do when they come across something inappropriate (inform their teacher or parent immediately).

Teach a lesson about Internet safety before any cell phone or Web 2.0 activity occurs. Instructing students to be mindful and aware during Internet and cell phone use should be part of all classroom learning in the 21st century. Parents may appreciate that their children are learning how to use the Internet and their cell phones appropriately, since parents are often uncertain how to teach their kids to use these new resources. Additionally, some Web sites (such as Phonezoo) have "family filters" that can be used to eliminate inappropriate advertising for children.

Web Publishing

Probably one of the largest concerns with using the Internet in schools is keeping our students safe from predators and harmful information. While school administrators spend much time creating acceptable use policies designed to let students know what they cannot do on the Internet (such as sending instant messages or e-mail), the policies often do not describe why students should not be participating in those collaborative activities. Not enough time is devoted to teaching our students how to safely participate in collaborative communities and to safely post media and text online. Students need to become digitally literate citizens and learn how to safely navigate these new Web 2.0 resources. Many students participate in social-networking sites such as MySpace, Facebook, and YouTube outside of school, with very little instruction on how to appropriately communicate in these worlds. By using cell phones, blogs, and other Web 2.0 resources for learning, we have an opportunity to teach students about the difference between public and private spaces on the Web; how to register or sign up for accounts; what information is appropriate for a profile; what types of images, text, and video can be published; where to find and change default settings; and how and when to communicate with others.

Publishing on the Web need not be a safety issue, because cell phone uploads can be kept private. Most Web 2.0 resources have private space that you can download to directly from your cell phone. This means that the student's work can stay private.

Once the material is in the private space, the teacher can decide whether to publish the student's work to the Web or to keep it private for classroom use. At the same time, there are opportunities to publish work on almost every Web 2.0 site, and students should be aware of why they would or would not select to publish to the Internet. One solution, if you want to publish the classroom work to share with others, is to talk with students about using pseudonyms for their names and to focus on content rather than personal information. For example, instead of recording a personal reflection with details of the their life, students can record their findings from a scientific experiment or debate a controversial issue.

Whenever students publish to the Web (especially using Web 2.0 resources and cell phones), you should get permission from the building administrator (and possibly the technology coordinator), inform parents, and have students sign a special permission form (in addition to the regular school acceptable use policy).

Getting Permission from Administrators

Before beginning the assignment, inform your principal and technology coordinator about your project idea. Always start small when you want to use something controversial like cell phones, by creating a project that is simple and can be completed outside the classroom, so that you are not asking administrators to change school policies that might ban or restrict cell phones on campus. Demonstrate how students will use cell phones with the Web resource (create a podcast or text message using your own cell phone that depicts what students will actually be doing). Show explicitly how the activity will align with content standards and other classroom goals (you could, for instance, address ISTE's National Educational Technology Standards for Students, the NETS•S). Finally, explain that the students and their parents will be signing special permission forms in order to participate and that you have an alternative assignment for anyone who cannot comply with the regulations or whose parents have concerns.

Writing the Permission Form

You may want to ask the district technology coordinator to help you write the permission form for the parents. Once the form has been written, I would recommend showing it to the school principal. Include the following points in the permission letter (see Figure 2.1 for a sample):

- Your excitement for the assignment.

- The administration's support of the assignment.

- The purpose of the assignment and generally how it will meet classroom goals.

- ISTE's NETS•S to demonstrate how the assignment addresses technology standards.

- Your intention to include instruction on Internet safety, publishing online, and cell phone etiquette as part of the assignment.

- Any costs that might be involved (for example, if you want students to text message, they might have to pay text-messaging fees if they do not have an unlimited plan). You may also want to include that you will ask students to educate themselves on their cell phone plans.

- Alternative options for students who do not have access to a cell phone (for example, they could use their parents' cell phone, a landline if it is a toll-free number, or a computer with a microphone).

- The consequences for students who misuse cell phones or Web 2.0 resources.

- The consequences for students who do not comply with the rules of the assignment.

- How public or private the project will be (for example, if the goal is to create cell phone podcasts that are posted online, will they be posted publicly or privately?). Explain what you are going to do to help protect the privacy and identities of students if the space is public (such as monitoring before posting or posting information that is content-based instead of personal).

- Your enthusiasm for parental participation in some form in the project (such as viewing the student-created podcasts and commenting on them).

- The links to sites you will use and any login protocol or passwords that parents would need to access their child's information.

- Your reasoning for the particular sites you selected.

- Your contact information for questions or concerns (and the administrator's).

- Your viewpoint that the assignment be considered a privilege.

Figure 2.1 Sample permission form

Dear Parents and Guardians:

We have an exciting new project that we will be starting in class this term. We are going to be creating a Poetry Slam Podcast. (A podcast is an audio broadcast over the Internet that can be played on an iPod, but also on any computer.) The purpose of this project is to allow students to create, recite, and publish their original poetry. Students will be creating poetry based on different genres. This project uses cell phones to create the podcasts in order to demonstrate how these devices can be used as a learning tool. As homework, outside of class, students will use their cell phones to record the podcasts. Alternatives will be provided for students without cell phones.

This project will not only meet our district language arts standards for original poetry but also the National Educational Technology Standards for Students (developed by the International Society for Technology in Education).

The podcast will be created using a free Web service called Gcast (www. gcast.com). I will be creating the class blog for the podcast and monitoring the posts using a Web application called Blogger (www.blogger.com/start/). Because the purpose of the assignment is to allow students to publish their work and receive feedback, the blog will be public. Students will be taught how to appropriately publish online and ways to protect their privacy. For safety, students will be using pseudonyms (as many famous authors have done, including Mark Twain, whose real name was Samuel Clemens). Additionally, we will be going over Internet safety protocol in class, and students will have to pass a quiz before they can participate in the project. (A sample Internet safety quiz can be found here: www.safekids.com/quiz/.)

I worked with the district technology coordinator to decide on the podcasting resource that would best fit our needs. Gcast allows us to use the resource for no cost and has a toll-free phone number so that students who do not have cell phone access can use a landline to do their podcasting.

Continued

Figure 2.1, *Continued*

I would like you to be able to view and comment on the students' poetry. Here is the link to the Poetry Slam Podcast Blog: www.poetryslam987.blogspot.com/.

The opportunity to use these learning resources is a privilege, and students will be given instructions on how to use these resources appropriately. If they abuse this privilege, they will be given an alternative assignment that does not involve cell phones or the Internet. Since we will be publishing the poetry and using cell phones, we would like your permission to allow your child to participate. We also ask that your child sign the agreement.

I _____

agree to allow my child _____
to participate in the Poetry Slam Podcast project.

I _____ agree to follow the rules for the Poetry
Slam Podcast project.

Parent's signature _____

Student's signature _____

If you have any questions or concerns, please do not hesitate to contact me or our building principal (he has approved the project). We think this is a wonderful opportunity for students to learn how to use their cell phones as educational tools as well as to learn about Internet safety and publishing information online. We hope that you will also participate in our project by viewing and commenting on the original poems.

Sincerely,

Liz Kolb
Eighth-Grade Language Arts Teacher
Anyschool
Contact Information Here

Student Permission and Agreement

While you can write a separate student permission form for students to agree to, I recommend getting the students involved in the process. Ask students to develop an agreement with you concerning the guidelines for the assignment. Of course, as the teacher, you make the final decision, but if you create a social contract with students, they are more likely to take ownership of and responsibility for the project. Once an agreement is made, have all students sign the social contract along with the permission form sent home to parents. Also, have students take an Internet or cell phone safety quiz before they participate in the project. (A good example of an Internet safety quiz is available at SafeKids: www.safekids.com/quiz/.) Items to discuss with students could include:

- **Safety.** How are we going to stay safe with online resources?

- **Etiquette.** How are we going to make sure that the cell phone activity is appropriate?

- **Responsibility.** What are the consequences for not complying?

- **Opportunity.** If this project goes well, students may suggest future cell phone assignments.

Security

Many educators consider cell phones to be not only a distraction in an instructional environment, but a security risk to the school itself. The National School Safety and Security Services (2007) cites the following reasons for banning cell phones in schools:

1. Cell phones have been used for calling in bomb threats to schools and, in many communities, cell calls cannot be traced by public safety officials.

2. Student use of cell phones could potentially detonate a real bomb if one is actually on campus.

3. Cell phone use by students can hamper rumor control and, in doing so, disrupt and delay effective public safety personnel response.

4. Cell phone use by students can impede public safety response by accelerating parental response to the scene of an emergency during times when officials may be attempting to evacuate students to another site.

5. Cell phone systems typically overload during a major crisis (as they did during the Columbine tragedy, World Trade Center attacks, etc.), and usage by a large number of students at once could add to the overload and knock out cell phone systems quicker than may normally occur. Since cell phones may be a backup communications tool for school administrators and crisis teams, widespread student use in a crisis could eliminate crisis team emergency communications tools in a very short period of critical time. (n.p.)

Although these are obvious concerns for cell phones in schools, keep in mind that students do not have to bring their cell phones into school in order to use them for class assignments. At the same time, cell phones can also be very beneficial in a school-related emergency crisis. For example, if a classroom does not have an analog phone and a student needs emergency medical care, a cell phone can be used to alert the office. If a student brings a weapon to school and threatens others students, someone could use a silent feature on a cell phone to quietly text message the authorities. If there is a fire or weather emergency in the school and a teacher is missing a student, the teacher can use a cell phone to call the student's cell phone. Again, this is another reason it is so important to educate students on how to appropriately use their cell phones in emergency situations. Fire and tornado drills at school teach students proper evacuation procedures; cell phones can and should be integrated as a part of the necessary procedures.

Additionally, the National Center for Missing and Exploited Children has set up wireless Amber Alerts (www.wirelessamberalerts.org). When an alert occurs in the area code of the cell phone, the cell phone user will get a text message about the missing child. According to the National Center for Missing and Exploited Children (2006), the first three hours that a child goes missing are critical to recovery of the child. Parents, teachers, and educators who are concerned about children's safety can sign up for free wireless Amber Alerts. Furthermore, schools can set up their own Amber Alert system for community members and parents if a student goes missing while walking to or from school or during recess.

Chapter 3

Cell Phone Podcasting, Voice Mail, Conferencing, and Mobile Notes

Internet podcasting is popular in today's culture, and people of all ages and interests are listening to and creating podcasts. According to Wikipedia (2006), "A podcast is a multimedia file distributed over the Internet using syndication feeds, for playback on mobile devices and personal computers" (n.p.). Basically, it is an audio broadcast on the Internet that can be downloaded to a portable MP3 player. Over the last couple of years, the use of podcasting for classroom learning has seen a slow rise. Although more and more teachers are becoming aware of the existence of podcasts, many of them are uncertain how to create their own classroom podcasts.

Some teachers assume that creating their own podcast is a daunting and time-consuming task. Technology-savvy teachers create podcasts with iPod, iMovie, GarageBand, or other software. These can be complex programs to use; for example, teachers often have to worry about uploading to a server, learning how to use the specific tool, and storing the podcasting audio files. Most teachers would like an even simpler solution. Cell phones may be the answer.

With the emergence of Web 2.0, we've seen a new generation of Web-based software that emphasizes online collaboration among users (O'Reilly, 2005). A handful of Internet resources allow you to talk into your cell phone and immediately record the narrative as a podcast to a Web site. In other words, you can create an instant podcast with one phone call. Using cell phones to create podcasts eliminates the need for external MP3 players, complex video- or audio-editing tools, or even uploading to the Internet. Cell phones coupled with simple and free Web resources do the work for you.

One venture that uses this technology is the Murmur project (http://murmurtoronto. ca), an oral history endeavor in which people use their cell phones to conduct on-location interviews about different cities around the world. The Murmur project captures stories about people, places, and events from that city by conducting cell phone interviews "on the street" in that particular city. It is a great way to capture oral histories, since people can often remember their experiences better when they are physically looking at the location where the event took place. Another educational project that uses cell phones as audio recorders is audioTagger (www.moolab.net/mobile/audioTagger.shtml), which captures sonic sounds from anywhere in the world. This would be an innovative project for physical science students who are studying sound waves, frequency, and pitch.

The next few pages describe six online resources for posting audio to the Internet with cell phones. The first three can be used to create instant podcasts on the Internet: Gabcast (www.gabcast.com), Gcast (www.gcast.com), and Hipcast (www.hipcast.com). Each resource utilizes cell phones to create innovative learning opportunities. All three sites allow users to store, post, and publish podcasts immediately after recording on a cell phone. They also have options for embedding the podcasts into Web sites and blogs. In addition, each includes RSS (Rich Site Summary or Really Simple Syndication) feeds and subscription links to the podcasts (so that you do not need your own blog or Web site to publish and circulate your podcast).

The remaining three online resources allow you to use your cell phone for Internet-accessible voice mail, phone conferencing, and mobile note taking. YouMail (www.youmail.com) allows anyone to create a free, immediate voice-mail account that posts to a private space on the Internet. Using a local cell phone number, students can call in and hear unique voice-mail greetings (which could be assignment or quiz instructions), and they can immediately record an audio file that posts to a voice-mail system, which can be accessed through the Internet or a cell phone as an MP3 file. As you will see in Lesson Plan 3, the free voice-mail system coupled with cell phones can be powerful tools for learning. Another free site, FreeConferencePro (www.freeconferencepro.com), allows many people to participate in a conference that can be recorded as a downloadable MP3 file. The site provides easy conferencing options for students and parents. Jott (www.jott.com) is another free resource that allows anyone to use a cell phone to create speech-to-text e-mails.

Included in this chapter are step-by-step tutorials demonstrating how to set up accounts and create podcasts, conferences, voice mails, and mobile notes with these six resources. Although none of these Internet sites was created specifically for the classroom, they can easily be molded into learning resources. In addition, this chapter describes a variety of methods in which secondary teachers can take advantage of these resources for constructive learning activities. In addition, three educators are highlighted, one elementary school, one middle school, and one high school teacher, who are currently using these resources in their classrooms.

Podcasting

Gabcast

Gabcast (www.gabcast.com) is a Web site that allows you to upload audio files and distribute them as podcasts. After you create a free account in Gabcast, you can set up one or many podcasting channels. People can subscribe to the channel and listen to the audio posts. In addition, Gabcast enables you to post a cell phone audio recording directly to your Gabcast channel. Any cell phone can be used to post to the same podcasting channel. This is a nice feature for teachers who want different students to publish podcasts on one podcasting channel. Teachers need to set up only one channel for the entire class to use. Each channel automatically has an RSS feed and subscription options for the audience. This means that parents, students, and community members can easily find and listen to the channel.

To create the podcast, the user simply dials the toll-free Gabcast number, follows the verbal directions, and records an audio podcast. Selecting the pound key on the cell phone immediately saves the recording, and it is automatically posted allows recording of any conference with no time limit. The person who creates the account can host as many conferences as he or she likes. Once you set up an account, you are given a special phone number to call with a code that you can provide to anyone you would like to participate in your conference. The host can also control the conference with options such as muting or ending user participation in the conference. Once the conference is finished, an MP3 file of the conference will appear in the host's FreeConferencePro account. The MP3 file is private until the account holder decides to make it public. The MP3 file can be downloaded, e-mailed, or loaded onto a Web page. Because FreeConferencePro does not have a time limit, it is a much better conferencing option than Gabcast. Lesson Plan 4: Virtual Science Symposium is a secondary science project that includes step-by-step instructions on how to use FreeConferencePro.

Mobile Notes

Jott

Jott (www.jott.com) is a free Web resource that allows anyone to use a cell phone to create mobile notes. Using Jott, a person can instantly create speech-to-text e-mails from a cell phone. You do not have to pay to send text messages as e-mails from your cell phone using Jott. Instead of typing text messages into your cell phone— an operation that can be costly and clumsy (especially for those not used to the process)—you dial a number and speak your e-mail (or text message). Jott's voice recognition instantly turns it into text for yourself or anyone else you choose. You can use Jott to send mass e-mail reminders to a large group of people. Immediately, I thought students with visual impairments would benefit from this resource.

The Jott messages are immediately e-mailed to the person or persons of your choice. They are also archived and saved on the Jott Web site in a private, secure area. This provides users with a record of all the messages sent. Jott allows students to use a cell phone to complete homework assignments outside of class (such as oral foreign language assignments) and send the message directly to the teacher. The next day in class, students do not need to bring their cell phone to access their assignment. They can log in to the Jott site on a classroom computer to listen to their audio recording or check their e-mail to read the transcribed text from the audio.

Jott also has a feature called Jott Links, which allows anyone to send a speech-to-text message to a third-party application such as Blogger, Google Calendar, or

LiveJournal. For instance, if I want to add an event to my Google Calendar, I can simply use my cell phone to call Jott and speak my event. Jott will automatically put a text version of the audio file on my Google Calendar. It will do the same for Blogger and LiveJournal. While Gabcast creates an MP3 podcast on a blog, Jott creates a new text post.

Some may argue that students could just send e-mail messages, but many secondary students still do not have Internet access at home. However, they often have a cell phone with them, allowing them to complete their homework assignments from anywhere using Jott. Although students can make quick audio recordings on their cell phones without Jott, most basic cell phones do not have the ability to transcribe those audio recordings into text messages. While this can be a useful organizational tool for most students, students with visual impairments may find it helps them better participate in written assignments and group projects such as a group blog. For example, students with visual impairments could use Jott Links to create an automatic text post on Blogger by speaking into their cell phone. Also, students who are practicing their English language skills, such as ESL students, may find Jott a useful tool to help them practice, since Jott will do a better speech-to-text transcription when English is enunciated properly. Lesson Plan 5: Physics Sound Waves includes a step-by-step tutorial on how to use Jott.

Table 3.1 summarizes the features of the six Web 2.0 resources discussed in this chapter.

Table 3.1 Comparison of Web 2.0 resources that provide podcasting, voice mail, conferencing, and mobile notes

	Gabcast	Gcast	Hipcast	YouMail	FreeConferencePro	Jott
Cost			✓			
Conference podcasting	✓				✓	
Toll-free phone number	✓	✓		✓		✓
Immediate posting to blog	✓		✓			
RSS feed	✓	✓	✓			
User can create playlists		✓	✓			
Export options (MP3, embed to blog or Web site, send to e-mail)	✓	✓	✓	✓	✓	✓
Private space available for unpublished work	✓	✓	✓	✓	✓	✓
Teacher can post greetings that students will hear when they dial in				✓	✓	

Data Collection

In many science and social studies classes, data collection is an important part of the learning process. Students are often asked to conduct and write their own research studies (such as a history term paper based on primary resources, or a science fair project). The research and data gathering for these studies are primarily done outside the classroom. Jott could be a helpful resource for teachers keeping track of student progress or for students compiling data. Instead of the traditional way of using note cards to document a fact or idea for a paper (resulting in hundreds of note cards), students could use their cell phone as a dictation device and record their thoughts and research as it happens. Because each Jott note is automatically saved in the Jott account online, they have an instant backup and do not have to worry about losing the information. Because it is quicker to dictate the notes than to write or type them, this allows for a quicker research process. Further, students could send an immediate Jott message to their teacher's e-mail if they have a question about their research. Although they could do this with a computer connected to the Internet, not all students have their own computer and Internet access outside of school. If their research is being conducted on location at a historical setting or a scientific site (such as a pond), a laptop might not be an option. However, it is rare for secondary students to be away from their cell phones!

Finally, because Jott automatically transcribes the audio messages into text, students could copy and paste their Jott e-mailed text right into the first draft of their research paper. In doing so, students would be able to edit their Jott notes into proper English for their papers.

Students with Special Needs

Using the Internet can be difficult for students who experience visual or kinesthetic impediments to navigation. Certain devices and software can help level the playing field for these students. However, they can be expensive and often force students to be labeled more than they usually are in the classroom. Students with visual impairments or kinesthetic disabilities can take advantage of the audio input features of cell phones and Web 2.0 sites to better participate in regular class assignments. For example, using Gabcast they can verbally record journal reflections or participate in other assignments that may require writing online (such as a blog journal or e-mail). Instead of having a written journal, students with visual impairments can have an online journal with audio reflections. Because Gabcast also has a private area, students do not have to have a published journal.

Using Jott, students with visual impairments can better participate in social class activities. They can communicate by using their cell phones to speak their messages to their group members or to record their data findings. In addition, because the Jott message turns into a text e-mail as well as audio, it allows students with visual impairments to dictate their written work from a cell phone. English as a second language students could use Jott to practice their English-speaking skills for homework and then immediately e-mail their audio sessions to their ESL teacher to receive feedback. Students of all ages who are struggling with speech impediments can use the privacy of podcasts to practice, hear themselves, and receive feedback from their teacher or speech therapist.

Teachers Who Podcast

Although using cell phones as learning tools is a new concept, some innovative teachers are already utilizing cell phones as part of their classroom instruction. The next few pages describe three examples, one elementary, one middle school, and one secondary, of using cell phones coupled with Web-based resources to create classroom podcasts.

Pat Sattler, a K–8 technology integration specialist in Michigan, developed "radio theatre" using Gcast (www.stjosephschooltrenton.com/podcasts/halloween_theater1.htm). Figure 3.1 shows a picture of her students' Halloween Radio Theatre podcast page. Sattler had students in Grades 4–8 contribute to the podcast. She used a single cell phone with all of her students to create her radio theater podcast.

This demonstrates that even a single cell phone in the classroom can be an innovative learning tool. In addition, using just one cell phone gave her more control over what can be a distracting device. The students created their own sound effects on Gcast. Sattler edited the playlist and then went on to embed the Gcast podcast player into her school's Web site by using Gcast's embed

Figure 3.1 Pat Sattler's radio theater podcast

Lesson Plan 1 ▪ Oral History Project

Content Area	Social studies
Grade Level	9–12
Tools	Gabcast, Blogger, and cell phones
Cost	Free
Standards	NETS•S Performance Indicators for Grades 9–12: 7, 8, 9, 10
	NCSS Standards: II, IV

Lesson Description

Students use cell phones and Gabcast to record, document, and publish an oral-history project. Each student will conduct an interview with a local community member who has lived through a significant historical event (such as a war, the civil rights movement, the Kennedy assassination, 9/11, or voting for the first time). After students conduct their interview and record it on their cell phone, they will immediately post their interview to a blog. Students can further develop their blog around their interview.

Process

In Class

1. Students select for an interview a local community member who has lived through or participated in a significant historical event (teachers can have a list for students to choose from).

2. Students research the event that their interviewee was involved in.

3. Students develop a list of questions to ask their interviewee.

4. Students set up a blog on Blogger that will be the destination of the interview. Step-by-step instructions for creating a blog follow.

A. Students go to Blogger at www.blogger.com.

B. Students click on *CREATE YOUR BLOG NOW.*

C. Students go through a menu of options to fill in information. They continue until they get to the blog's editing window (it should look like the one to the left).

5. Students add an introductory post to their blog. This post describes who they are interviewing and why. Simply follow these directions:

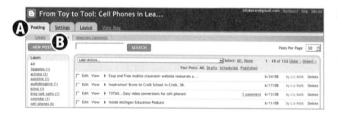

A. To create an introductory post, students click on the *Posting* tab in the editing window.

B. In the Posting window, students click on the *Create* link.

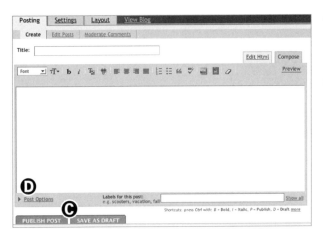

C. In the Create window, students can type their introductory message and choose *Save as Draft* or *Publish Post*.

D. Students can select to allow people to comment on the post under *Post Options*.

E. Once students click on the orange *Publish Post* button, they will be brought to a window where they can view their blog with the new post.

F. In this status window, students can click on *View Blog* to see their blog.

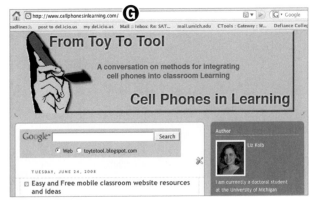

G. Notice that when the site opens, the Web address for the students' site will appear in the URL space. This is the site address students can give to people who want to view their blog.

6. Students create an account in Gabcast that publishes cell phone podcasts immediately to their blog. Please note that students will need an e-mail account to sign up for Gabcast. If schools do not allow e-mail, then the teacher can set up the Gabcast accounts using a filtered e-mail service such as Gaggle (http://gaggle. net). Here is how students (or the teacher) can set up their Gabcast account.

A. Students go to Gabcast at www.gabcast.com.

B. Students click on *Sign Up* for a free account.

C. Students should agree to the terms and conditions of service and verify their age.

D. Have students complete the registration form. (The screen name does not have to be the student's real name. They don't need to have an image.)

E. After they select *Submit*, students will have to go to their e-mail to confirm their account.

7. Once the Gabcast account has been confirmed, students can set up their own podcast channel for the interview. Here is how:

A. Have students click on *My Channels.*

B. Then students click on *Create a new channel.*

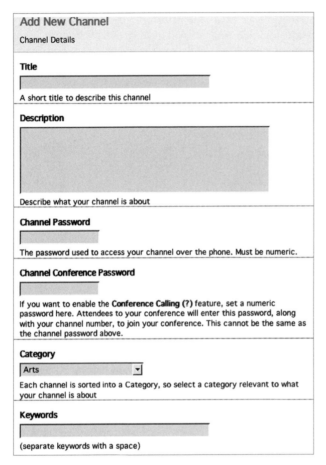

C. Have students go through the process to create the channel.

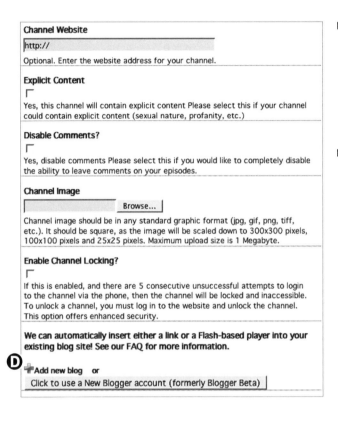

D. To post the interview podcast directly to their blog site, students can select the *Add new blog* button and put in their blog information. As a result, when they publish their interview (or interviews) they will automatically embed into their blog site.

E. Now students click on the *Submit* button at the bottom of the page.

8. Once their channel is set up, students copy down the channel information to record their podcast. Follow these instructions:

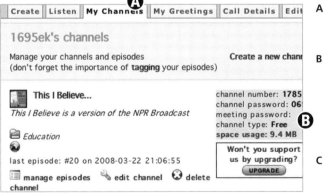

A. Students click on *My Channels* to see their channel information.

B. In their channel window, students should have a channel number and channel password. They should copy down the number and password so they have it when they call in for the interview.

C. Now students are ready to call in and record their podcast interview!

Outside Class

9. Students contact their interviewee and set up a time for the interview.

10. Students bring their cell phone, their Gabcast channel number, and their Gabcast channel password to the interview.

11. Students call the toll-free Gabcast number: 1-800-749-0632.

12. Students listen to the instructions (it will ask for the channel number and the channel password).

13. Students press the number 1 on the cell phone to start recording the interview. They then place the cell phone on the desk and start the interview. Students have up to 60 minutes of recording time in Gabcast. If they need more time, they can make a second recording.

14. Be sure students press the pound sign (#) when they finish recording and the number 2 to publish to their blog on Blogger. If they do not hit the number 2, their interview recording will still be saved to Gabcast as an unpublished file, but it will not yet be published to the blog.

Back in Class

15. Students can check their blogs to make sure their Gabcast interviews posted (they should have posted directly to the blogs on Blogger). Students type in their Blogger URL address to check their blog.

16. If the interview did not post, students can log back in to their Gabcast account and post it from there. Here is how:

A. Have students log in to their Gabcast account at http://gabcast.com.

B. In Gabcast, students click on *My Channels.*

C. Students click on *manage episodes.*

D. In the manage episodes window, students click on *player html.*

E. In the player html window, students click on *Highlight Text.*

F. Students go to the *Edit* menu in their browser and copy the text (or right-click and copy the text).

G. Students can now exit out of Gabcast.

H. Students log in to their Blogger account at http://blogger.com.

I. Students click on *Create new post.*

J. In their new post window, students click on *Edit Html.*

K. Now students paste in their player code, so it looks like the one to the left.

L. Students click on *PUBLISH POST.*

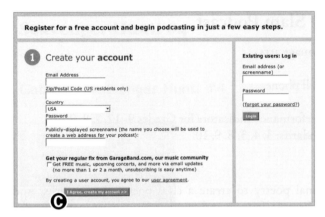

C. Put in your e-mail address, ZIP code, a username (such as Liz), and a password. (Teachers do not have to use their real information, except for the e-mail.) Click on *I Agree, create my account.*

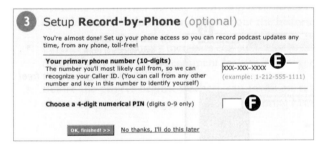

D. You will now select a podcast name (it can be a topic like Poetry Slam or your class name). Write a short description. Then click on *Next*.

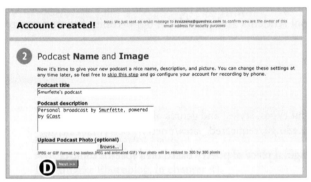

E. Put in a primary phone number. It does not have to be your real number, just a 10-digit number that students will remember. Students will need this when they call in to create an audio post.

F. Select an easy-to-remember PIN (personal identification number). Students will need this when they call in to create an audio post.

Outside Class

4. The teacher gives to students the primary phone number and PIN used to set up the class Gcast account so that students can use these when they call in to Gcast.

5. Students dial the Gcast toll-free number on their cell phone or landline: 1-888-654-2278.

6. Students follow the audio instructions (they will be asked to provide the primary phone number and PIN).

7. The recording will begin. Students recite their poems using their cell phone or a landline.

8. When they finish recording, students must press the pound sign (#) to post.

9. Students' podcasts should have automatically posted to Gcast. To check, they can log in to Gcast at home or wait for the next class.

Back in Class

10. In class, the teacher or students can log in to Gcast to see if the podcasts posted. Here is how:

A. Log in to the class Gcast account at www.gcast.com. Once in Gcast, the teacher or students can check for their podcasts under the Master Playlist.

11. The teacher or students can now put the poems in order on a playlist. Here is how:

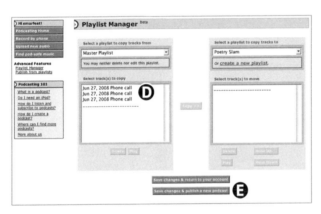

A. The teacher or students select *you can create a new playlist.*

B. The teacher or students can create a description of the poems (or if students had poems on different topics, more than one playlist can be created, one for each topic).

C Once the playlist name and description have been established, click on *Save changes to playlist.*

D. Now the teacher or students can select the poetic recitations that they want to have on that playlist and the order.

E. Once the playlist has been developed, click on *Save changes & publish a new podcast.*

12. Teachers, students, and other interested parties can view and listen to the published podcast. Here is how:

A. Back in the teacher's account, click on the name of the class podcast to see the published Poetry Slam Podcast page.

B. The teacher and students should be able to view the new podcast playlist and listen to it. This is the public page that family, friends, and community members can access to listen to the class podcasts. In addition, images and descriptions can be added about the poems in the podcasts.

C. Viewers can use the RSS feed to subscribe to the class poetry slam as well. They simply click on *Get future podcast episodes* and select which feed they like. With the RSS feed they do not have to log back in to the Gcast page to listen to the future class poetry slams.

Extensions

- The teacher can also set up a blog with Blogger (http://blogger.com), where all the students will post their Gcast poetry (see Blogger tutorial in Lesson Plan 1). The blog could also include images to represent the original poems.

- Students could set up their own individual Gcast poetry podcast accounts instead of having a class account. In their individual accounts, students could publish their own original poetry and short stories throughout the entire term.

- Since Gcast is toll-free, students can use a landline if they do not have access to a cell phone or are concerned about cell phone minutes.

- Teachers could invite a poet to introduce or participate in the poetry slam.

- To help motivate the students, teachers could also create a "competition" in which community members vote on their favorite poem in the slam.

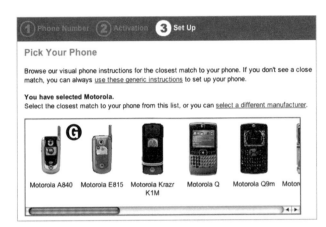

G. Select your cell phone model, and click on *Continue*.

H. Follow the tutorial on how to set up your new YouMail voice mail on your particular phone. (If you later decide that you do not want to use YouMail as your voice mail, you can always go back to your old service.)

I. When you finish, you will be brought to the YouMail message center.

2. The teacher should now ask students to call the teacher's cell phone number so that student numbers can be added to the contact list (this could be done for homework). Here is how:

A. Students should dial the teacher's cell phone number and leave any message.

B. Once they have left a message, it will show up in the teacher's YouMail account online.

C. The teacher should log in to the YouMail account and click on *Voicemail*.

D. The new messages should all show up here. Now the teacher should click on *More actions* and choose *Add callers as contacts*.

E. The teacher should insert the student's proper name, then click on *Create Contacts*.

F. Create a new group by clicking on *Click here to add a new group*.

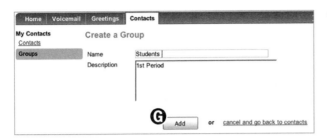

G. Name the group appropriately and provide a description (such as "students" or "1st Period"). Once you finish, click on *Add*.

H. Now you can add new contacts to the group by putting a check by the students you want to add to the group (you can make multiple groups for multiple class periods). Once you are finished, click on *Save*.

3. The teacher sets up the quiz instructions by changing the voice-mail greeting. Here is how:

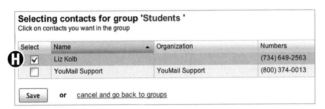

A. Go to YouMail at http://youmail.com.

B. Log in to your account (use your phone number and the PIN you were given).

C. Click on the Greetings tab. Under *Actions*, click on *Record*.

D. In Record a Greeting, name your greeting (so you remember the assignment name).

E. If you have a built-in microphone you can select to use the online recorder.

F. Record your greeting (the assignment), and then select *Save and pick who hears.*

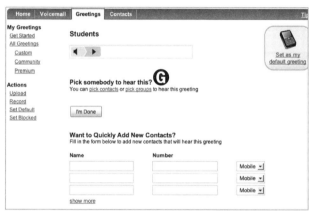

G. Now you can assign your greeting to the appropriate group of students by clicking on the *pick groups* link under Pick somebody to hear this?

H. Select the group or groups of students whom you want to complete the assignment.

I. Click on *Save.*

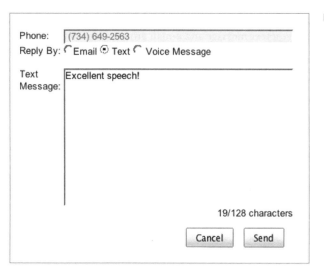

F. In addition, you can text message the students to give them feedback by selecting the person and then clicking on *Reply* (a window will open like the one to the left).

Method 2: To listen to the voice-mails quizzes on a cell phone.

A. Call your cell phone voice mail or dial 1-714-204-3114 (the number to YouMail) from your cell phone.

Extensions

- Instead of providing written feedback, the teacher can record student evaluations using a cell phone. (The evaluation can be in the foreign language to provide more listening practice for students.) After listening to a student's message on a cell phone, the teacher can press 88 and record a greeting (feedback) specifically for that student.

- Teachers can also use YouMail to save the oral quizzes over the entire semester and document the improvement of the students.

- This lesson plan also works well for English as a second language students.

- Students could create quizzes with YouMail by setting up their own accounts and a message. This would also be a good way for students to practice their oral language skills. Each month a different student or students could be in charge of creating the oral quiz instructions on YouMail.

Lesson Plan 4 ▪ Virtual Science Symposium

Content Area	Science
Grade Level	9–12
Tools	FreeConferencePro and cell phones
Cost	Free
Standards	NETS•S Performance Indicators for Grades 9–12: 7, 8, 9, 10
	NSES Standards: Science in Personal and Social Perspectives
	Content Standard F: Grades 9–12

Lesson Description

Students in two different schools will participate in joint virtual cell phone conferences concerning topical issues in science. Topical issues include stem cell research, nutrition, global warming, genetically engineered foods, and cloning, to name a few. Students will be placed in groups of five, in which two students from one school will be paired with two students from another school; the remaining student (from either school) will be the moderator or host of the conference. Each student in the group will research and "become" a well-known scientist in a specific field. The students will take on their scientist's perspective on the issue and participate in a virtual conference for homework. The virtual conferences will be automatically saved as an MP3 file with the assistance of FreeConferencePro.

Process

In Class

1. Two teachers from different schools in the same or a similar science subject area pair up and decide on the topical issues they want their students to discuss.

2. Each teacher assigns two students to each agreed-upon controversial topic.

3. In their groups, the students select current or past scientists who have contributed to a specific controversial scientific topic.

4. Students research their particular scientist and the scientist's perspective on the topic.

5. The teachers select one additional student to become the moderator or host for the group. This student records the conference and asks questions to keep the conference flowing. This student also develops a list of questions for the virtual symposium.

6. One of the teachers sets up a FreeConferencePro account. Here is how:

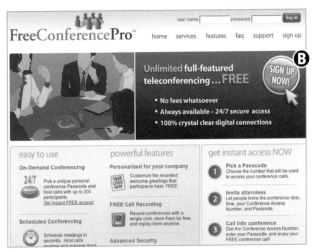

A. Go to FreeConferencePro at http://freeconferencepro.com.

B. Click on *SIGN UP NOW.*

C. Fill in the appropriate information and click on *submit.*

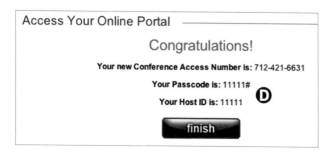

D. A new screen will appear with the conference access number, the passcode, and the host ID. Copy down all three of these numbers. Students will use the conference phone number and passcode to access the conference from their cell phones. The host student can use the host ID to start and stop and control the conference.

E. Now the teacher can set up an online portal (this is where teachers will be able to download the MP3 conference sessions).

7. The teachers give their students the conference phone number and the passcode. They also give the host students the host ID.

Outside Class

8. Students in each group select a mutual time to conference for homework.

9. The host student dials in to the conference phone number, types in the passcode, and presses the asterisk (*) symbol.

10. The host will then be asked to type in the host ID. Once the host ID has been entered, the host should select the pound sign (#) and number 9. This will start the conference recording.

11. The rest of the students can now dial in to the conference phone number.

12. Students should type in the passcode followed by the pound sign (#).

13. Once all the students in the group are on the conference line, they can begin the conference.

14. When the conference is done, the students can just hang up.

Back in Class

15. For the teachers to listen to and evaluate the conferences (or share them with the rest of the class), they have to log in to the FreeConferencePro portal. Here is how:

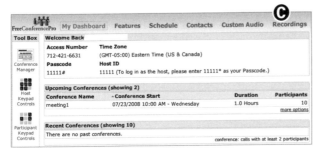

A. Log in to FreeConferencePro at http://freeconferencepro.com.

B. Sign in to the portal account. The portal account shows when conferences were recorded and how long they lasted.

C. Click on *Recordings*.

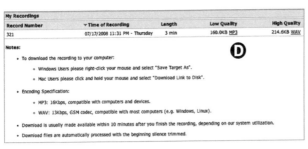

D. In the Recordings window, teachers can download an MP3 file of the conferences. There is also an option to listen to recordings over the phone.

Extensions

- If you do not have another school or classroom to pair up with, your students can participate with students in other class periods of the same subject that you teach.

- Teachers can ask an expert scientist from the local community (or really anywhere) to participate in the virtual conferences.

- The virtual conferences can be posted on the class blog or Web page so that other students can listen to them and parents can listen and comment.

- Teachers can also participate in the conference sessions.

- Instead of doing the conference sessions all at once, a conference could be conducted about once a month (or at the beginning of each new unit, as an introduction for that topic). Each group of students would be in charge of the conference for only one month (or unit) during the school year.

Lesson Plan 5 ▪ Physics Sound Waves

Content Area	Physics
Grade Level	9–12
Tools	Jott, Audacity, and cell phones
Cost	Free
Standards	NETS•S Performance Indicators for Grades 9–12: 7, 8, 9, 10
	NSES Standards: Physical Science

Content Standard B: Grades 9–12

- Structure and properties of matter
- Motions and forces
- Interactions of Energy and Matter

Lesson Description

This activity is an introduction to studying sound in a physics course. Using Jott and their cell phones, students will record different sounds they hear in their everyday life. Students will use Audacity to explore the sounds and investigate physics concepts such as pitch, frequency, sound waves, speed of sound waves, and octave. Audacity is a free audio-editing tool for both Windows and Macintosh computers that can be downloaded at http://audacity.sourceforge.net.

Process

In Class

1. Each student sets up a personal Jott account. (Please note that students will need to have their own e-mail accounts to confirm their Jott registration. If schools have a policy against students using generic e-mail, teachers can set up monitored and safe e-mail accounts for the students at Gaggle, http://gaggle.net, or the teacher can set up the Jott accounts.) Here is how to set up the accounts:

A. Students go to Jott at http://jott.com.

B. Students click on *SIGN UP FOR A FREE ACCOUNT.*

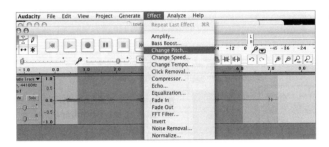

A. In Audacity, students can go to the *Effect* menu to adjust and work with pitch and other sound wave options.

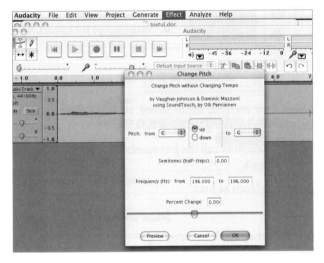

Extensions

- Students could be assigned specific sounds to find in the real world (such as vocal sounds, automotive sounds, or natural sounds).

- Groups of students could focus on one sound concept, such as pitch, and then present their pitch research to the rest of the class with the assistance of Audacity.

Chapter 4

Cell Phones as Cameras and Camcorders

Recording audio with a cell phone is only one way to use this digital device for instruction. This chapter describes how cell phones can be used as collection and storage devices for photos and videos. For school districts that are fortunate enough to own digital camcorders and cameras (and all the associated accessories such as tripods, DV tapes, and microphones), it is often difficult to manage this expensive equipment. In addition, educators are hesitant to allow students to take the equipment home for school projects. Consequently, the projects need to be done during valuable class time or educators need to rely on students independently finding the expensive digital equipment to conduct video and still-image projects. Cell phones provide a solution.

Cell phones with cameras and camcorders are in fact becoming common, and thus it is important to consider some innovative uses of these features. Further, every year more Web sites emerge that allow people to upload, edit, and present their digital photos and videos. Web sites such as Flickr and YouTube have become extremely popular for sharing photos and videos. Some of these Web sites allow participants to "go mobile" and immediately upload pictures and videos taken on their cell phone to the Web site. Although educators may worry about uploading digital images and video directly to the Internet, most of these Web sites offer a private space for digital media. Many of these resources have their own free online image and video editors. As a result, classroom projects that are usually done with Photoshop, iMovie, or Movie Maker can now be completed online at any computer at any time.

Free online resources that can be coupled with cell phones to create engaging visual classroom projects include Blogger (www.blogger.com), Photobucket (http://photobucket.com), Flickr (http://flickr.com), Flagr (http://flagr.com), YouTube (http://youtube.com), blip.tv (http://blip.tv), and Eyespot (http://Eyespot.com). All of these resources allow users to directly post and publish images and videos captured with a cell phone. The lesson plans in this chapter provide many examples of how to harness these resources for learning activities outside the classroom.

Cell Phones as Cameras

Whereas just about every secondary subject area relies on visual images at some point in the learning process, schools often lack the resources for students to take their own images (such as having enough digital cameras for every student to use). Almost all cell phones come equipped with a camera, and the quality of the camera has greatly improved over the last few years. Consequently, most students have an image-capturing device with them at all times. This ubiquitous tool used in concert with Internet resources presents opportunities for students to extend their learning beyond the classroom. In the following sections I describe four free Web 2.0 resources that can be used with a cell phone to capture and manage visual images: Blogger, Photobucket, Flagr, and Flickr.

Blogger

Blogging has become an extremely popular social activity in youth culture over the last couple of years, and is also developing into a useful tool in education. Cell phones can enhance the learning experiences with blogs in the classroom by adding photoblogs and audioblogs. In the previous chapter, we looked at how podcasts could be added to a blog. Blogger (www.blogger.com), one of the most popular blogging resources, has a feature that allows anyone with a camera phone to take pictures and immediately post them to a Blogger blog. The Blogger photoblog is public, which means that the photos posted will immediately be visible to anyone who is surfing the Internet.

Although some teachers may worry about the blog being public, remember that the purpose of a blog is to create a Web journal that is published. Therefore, it is important to let your students know that they will be publishing their photos and should be aware of the types of images they are posting. Chapter 7 addresses Internet safety issues. If you do not want your students posting directly to a public space on the Internet, then you may want to consider using one of the photo-capturing resources that does have private space, such as Photobucket or Flickr.

The benefit of using Blogger for photoblogging is that you do not have to have a Blogger blog in order to photoblog. For instance, if you are on a field trip with your students, and decide to take pictures of the experience, you can photoblog without having previously set up a blog. You can set up the blog directly from your cell phone. Lesson Plan 6: Local Landmarks Photoblog is a social studies activity that includes step-by-step instructions for creating a Blogger photoblog.

Photobucket

Similar to Blogger, Photobucket (http://photobucket.com) enables anyone to post pictures to the Web from a cell phone. Whereas in Blogger the images immediately become public, in Photobucket you can post directly into your private space. Additionally, Photobucket allows photo postings from any cell phone to one account by giving out a unique e-mail address for the account. This is a useful feature for classroom teachers who want to set up one Photobucket account for the entire class to post to from their individual cell phones. It allows teachers to have more control over the photo postings (teachers can delete or edit posted photos before anyone else can see them). If your cell phone has a camcorder, you can also send video to the private Photobucket account.

Unique to Photobucket is a feature that allows users to edit their pictures online to create picture slide shows or "remixes," which are essentially movies made with the uploaded photos and videos. Similar to iMovie or Movie Maker, you can insert audio, transitions, effects, and titles into the remix videos. You can post your slide shows to a blog or Web site or you can e-mail them. These slide shows are easy, fun, and engaging projects for students. Lesson Plan 7: Geometry Digital Storybook includes a step-by-step tutorial on using Photobucket with cell phones.

Flickr

Flickr (http://flickr.com) is a popular free photo-sharing site that allows users to keep images private or share them with the world. Most people put pictures on Flickr by uploading them from their computers. However, with Flickr you can also upload pictures directly from your cell phone. Similar to Photobucket, Flickr allows you to keep your photos private until you decide what you want to do with them. Once in Flickr, you can create simple slide shows, add tags, and provide descriptions for the images. Also, you get a personal Flickr e-mail address, where you can send pictures directly from any cell phone. This is wonderful for schools because teachers often want students to contribute to the same resource, and students can send pictures from any cell phone to the same Flickr account.

Flickr can link to many other Web 2.0 sites, which helps when integrating projects and activities. For example, Phixr (http://phixr.com) is a free photo-editing Web site that allows students to import photos directly from their Flickr account. It allows you to do many of the things you would be able to do with Adobe Photoshop, such as crop photos, change hues and saturation, and manipulate effects. Students can take images with their cell phone camera for homework, send them from their cell phone to their Flickr account, then back in school they can edit those photos in Phixr. Many other Web 2.0 sites also allow for importing from Flickr. Instead of having to purchase expensive photo-editing software, teachers can take advantage of these free photo-editing sites where students can work on their photos from anywhere. Lesson Plan 8: Rock Identification is a science activity that includes a step-by-step tutorial on using Flickr with cell phones. Lesson Plan 9: PhotoMapping also uses Flickr.

Flagr

Flagr (http://flagr.com) is a free Web 2.0 resource that allows people to post images to a specific location on a map using their mobile phone camera. One benefit of Flagr for schools is that unlike many mobile map-posting sites, which usually require cell phones to have GPS capabilities, Flagr allows posting from any basic cell phone that can text message. This means that any student who has a cell phone can participate in a Flagr map project.

Flagr allows private, semi-private, or public map postings. All three of these options work well for learning. The private map allows only one person to post to it. One example of using the private map would be a student documenting her spring break trip to Honduras. The semi-private map allows many students to post to one map as long as they have been invited by the map owner (most likely the teacher). The semi-private option is beneficial for class projects in which students identify and post local community features or biological phenomena, but you do not want the general public to post to the map, because you would like to see what the students can find on their own. The public map option is nice for classrooms studying cultural, historical, or scientific landmarks on a global scale. For example, if you teach Spanish class, you may want people from Spanish-speaking locations around the world to take pictures of their local cultural landmarks. If you are studying architecture, you may be interested in having public maps for different architectural styles, and asking people from around the world to contribute images of buildings with those particular styles. If students do not have a cell phone, Flagr has an option to post using a computer. Lesson Plan 10: Geo-Insects presents ideas on using Flagr in the science classroom.

Cell Phones as Camcorders

The latest cell phones now come with camcorders. Some educational groups are already taking advantage of these tiny camcorder phones by having online cell phone movie festivals, such as the CellFlix Festival (http://cellflixfestival.org), sponsored by Ithaca College, and Pocket Films Festival in Japan (www.pocketfilms.jp/en/). Many Web sites, such as YouTube and blip.tv, allow you to upload your homemade videos from your computer, creating an Internet-based TV channel, and share them with the public. While in the past some schools have been able to have their own broadcast TV channel through their local cable companies, it is often a costly and time-consuming venture. Additionally, schools are really only able to broadcast to the local community and do not reach a global audience. By creating an Internet-based broadcast channel, schools can reach a global audience and keep their costs down. Since these channels allow broadcasting from cell phones, students can become "roving" reporters and create broadcasts from anywhere in the world.

This can have a great effect on education because students no longer need to have access to iMovie, Movie Maker, or other video-editing software to edit their video recordings. Video footage takes up so much hard drive space that students often have to use a school computer to do their video-editing because home computers can't accommodate the files. This means students may have less time and less access to work on videos, and teachers often become concerned by the amount of time they must give students to use the computer to finish video editing. By employing online editing tools, students can log in to the Web site at any time, from any computer, and work on their videos. In addition, they can immediately post the final product online. No more worries about transferring to a DVD or compressing files. The following section describes YouTube, blip.tv, and Eyespot, three Web-based resources that can be used to create mobile TV channels.

YouTube and blip.tv

YouTube (http://youtube.com) and blip.tv (http://blip.tv) are free Web-based video-posting and video-sharing sites where you can upload your own movies into their giant movie database. Additionally, both of these sites allow video uploading from just about any cell phone that has a camcorder. These sites give members their own Internet-based TV channel that people can subscribe to. Both sites also allow you to immediately post a video from your cell phone to a third-party site, such as your own blog. While YouTube allows you to post videos privately, blip.tv automatically publishes the videos to the public, unless you purchase a "pro" account.

The ability to create your own TV channel using a cell phone has many potential applications for learning. For example, students in social studies with a focus on current events can create a TV show with local news. Students can create their mobile news reports for homework, which creates authentic reporting opportunities because they will be able to interact on location with community members. When they finish recording, they could publish the mobile broadcasts to the class blip.tv or YouTube channel. In a few years, students will be able to publish live broadcasts from just about any cell phone. Currently two sites—Qik (http://qik.com) and Flixwagon (http://flixwagon.com)—allow you to publish live broadcasts using a cell, but only with Nokia phones.

Eyespot

Eyespot (http://eyespot.com) is an online video-posting, video-sharing, and video-editing tool. It is a free site where you can upload pictures and small movie files; edit (by adding effects, transitions, titles, and even narration); then directly post pictures to a Web site or a blog, send to your e-mail, or download to your desktop. Eyespot also allows anyone to immediately post a video recording from a cell phone to the site. Even better, Eyespot has both a public and a private space, so students can store videos and photos and edit them in private.

After students finish their masterpieces, they have the option of publishing their work to the greater Eyespot community, where they can receive feedback. This would be fine for projects that do not have any personal identifiers. If teachers prefer that students not publish their videos to the general public, they can download the videos as QuickTime files from the private editing space on Eyespot. Lesson Plan 11: Telenovela is a foreign language activity that includes a step-by-step tutorial on using Eyespot and cell phones. Lesson Plan 12: Scavenger Hunt also uses Eyespot.

Table 4.1 summarizes the features of the Web 2.0 resources discussed in this chapter.

Table 4.1 Comparison of camera and camcorder Web 2.0 resources

	Blogger (photoblogging)	Photobucket	Flickr	Flagr	Eyespot	blip.tv	YouTube
Cost							
Private space		✓	✓	✓	✓		✓
Video posts from cell		✓			✓	✓	✓
Photo- or video-editing feature		✓	✓ (limited)		✓		
RSS feed	✓		✓			✓	✓
Ability to post to one space from any cell		✓	✓	✓		✓	
Export options		✓	✓	✓	✓	✓	✓

Classroom Use of Cell Phones as Cameras and Camcorders

Although it is helpful to know how to couple cell phones with Web 2.0 sites for image sharing, we also need to consider how to use these resources to create knowledge construction activities for the classroom. The following sections describe ways that cell phone cameras and camcorders can be used as learning tools for content-based activities. All of these activities can be conducted without bringing a cell phone into the classroom.

Data Collection

Often in earth and biological science research objects are taken out of their natural setting and brought into the classroom to study (such as leaves, soil, or animals). Students could demonstrate their knowledge of the different natural objects by finding them in their natural setting, taking pictures of them with their cell phones, and posting them to their own Blogger photoblog or a private class Flickr account. Students could text along with their picture a short description of what type of leaves, soil, or animal species they have captured. Allowing students to document the objects in their natural setting creates a more authentic assessment of student knowledge. Another example is having students grow plants for a science experiment. They could take pictures daily to monitor the growth of the plant and post the pictures directly to their Blogger blog or to Flickr. With the pictures easy to access, students can receive feedback about their science experiment at any time from the teacher.

Documentaries

Instead of lugging around expensive camcorders, microphones, DV tapes, and tripods, students have an "all-in-one" camcorder with their cell phone. Using their cell phone, students can record multiple interviews (of a local community leader or a grandparent, for instance) and immediately post the videos to Eyespot. Students can use the Eyespot editing tools to create a documentary, and they can edit the video on their own time rather than taking days or even weeks of valuable class time. When they finish, they can publish the documentary on their blog, send it to their teacher, or download it. Students can also receive feedback on their documentary from all over the world by publishing it on Eyespot or submitting it to a student film festival such as CellFlix.

Digital Audio-Narrated Storybooks

Digital storybooks have become popular in classroom learning for illustrating fiction and nonfiction stories. Instead of using a more complex video editor, students create their own simple digital storybook with Photobucket and a cell phone. Cell phones are also more convenient than scanners or cameras with cable hookups. Students can simply take pictures with their cell phones on a field trip, for homework, or in class, and immediately send the pictures to Photobucket. In Photobucket, students can use the simple video-editing remix tools to put together a digital storybook. The storybook editing and narration can be done as a homework assignment, which students can e-mail to their teacher or link to a blog when finished.

Digital Image Storybooks

With the assistance of Flickr, students can take pictures and tell a story with their cell phones. The story can be a documentary about a personal experience outside of school (such as learning something new, researching a content-based topic, or getting over a fear), or it could be a fictional story that they make up and illustrate with images from everyday life. Using their cell phones, students take pictures for their digital image stories and send them immediately to their private Flickr account. Once they have their pictures in Flickr, they create a slide show and write a description for each photo that tells the story. When finished, students can post the links to their digital image stories on the school Web site or send them in e-mails. Parents, teachers, and other students can then provide feedback on the digital image stories.

Clay Animation

Clay animation is a common way for students to demonstrate their understanding of scientific concepts, historical events, and literature, and to express original ideas. Instead of spending class time setting up their clay animation frames and taking pictures, students can use their cell phones outside of school to take pictures of the individual frames. After taking the pictures, students can post them to Eyespot and use the "trim" options of the Eyespot online video editor to change the timing of the pictures, so they run in a quick sequence for the animation. They can also add music, transitions, or text to their animations. When completed, the clay animation movies can be posted to the class Web site or simply downloaded to a classroom computer. When students create their clay animations mostly at home, parents can get involved and students will not feel constrained by a time limit.

News Broadcasts

Students can use their cell phone camcorders to record 30-second to 3-minute news broadcast segments that feature interviews with community members or footage of local or school events. In addition, they can take pictures of community events or personalities with the cell phone camera. The videos can be posted directly to Eyespot, blip.tv, or YouTube. In class, students can edit the videos using the Eyespot or Photobucket video editor or they can download and use iMovie or Movie Maker.

Lesson Plans

The following seven lesson plans illustrate how to use the camera and camcorder features of cell phones for learning. These secondary lesson plans span a variety of content areas and integrate the Web 2.0 resources mentioned in this chapter (Blogger, Photobucket, Flickr, Flagr, and Eyespot). These are just suggestions of how cell phones can be learning tools. Keep in mind that they all can be modified to fit a variety of classrooms and subject areas.

Lesson Plan 6   ▪   Local Landmarks Photoblog

Content Area   Social studies
Grade Levels   6–12
Tools   Blogger and cell phones
Cost   Free (text-messaging charges may apply)
Standards   NETS•S Performance Indicators for Grades 9–12: 7, 8, 9, 10
  NETS•S Performance Indicators for Grades 6–8: 5, 6, 7, 9
  NCSS Standards: I, II, III

Lesson Description

Students will each be in charge of learning about a local historical landmark (such as a veteran memorial, a historical home, or a statue or sculpture). They will each create a photoblog Web page that describes the significant features of the landmark.

Process

In Class

1. Students prepare for their excursions by researching local historical landmarks.

Outside Class

At their landmark, students take images and immediately post them to a Blogger blog (which they do not need to set up beforehand). Here is how:

2. Students visit their landmark.

3. Students take a picture of the landmark on their cell phone.

4. After they take the picture, students send the picture in a message from their phone to go@blogger.com. A Blogger blog will automatically be set up for them.

5. In a couple minutes, they will receive a message on their cell phone with a claim token and a URL link to their blog.

6. Now students can take as many pictures as they would like of their historical landmark. Any photos that students send to go@blogger.com will automatically post to their new blog.

Back in Class

7. Students look at their new blog with the URL link they were sent on their cell phone. Here is how:

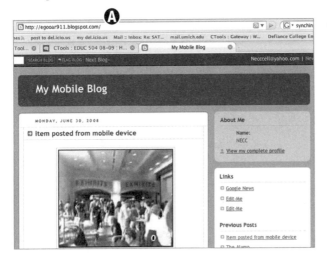

A. Students access the Internet and type in the URL for their blog (it should be in their cell phone message). All the pictures the students sent from their cell phones will be posted here.

8. Students can now claim their blog to edit it. Here is how:

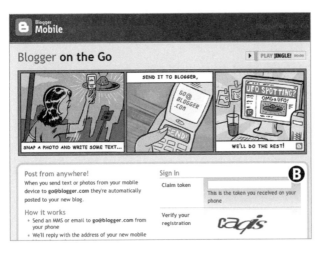

A. Students should note the claim token they received on their cell phones (they can copy this down and bring it with them to class).

B. Students log in to Blogger Mobile by going to www. blogger.com/mobile-start.g and typing in the claim token.

9. Students can now edit their Blogger blog by adding descriptions of the images, significant facts about the landmark, maps to the landmark, or links to other Web resources about the landmark.

Extensions

- Teachers could invite a historian from the local historical society to introduce the historical landmarks in the area.

- Students could offer to create a Web site for the local historical society where they could link to their blogs on local landmarks.

- Students could use Jott (see chapter 3) when they are visiting their local landmark to take audio mobile notes about significant facts and features. They could in turn insert their Jott text or audio into their Blogger photoblogs once they are back in class.

Lesson Plan 7 ▪ Geometry Digital Storybook

Content Area	Geometry
Grade Levels	6–8
Tools	Photobucket and cell phones
Cost	Free (text-messaging charges may apply)
Standards	NETS•S Performance Indicators for Grades 6–8: 5, 6, 7, 9

NCTM Geometry Standard for Grades 6–8:

• Analyze characteristics and properties of two- and three-dimensional geometric shapes and develop mathematical arguments about geometric relationships.

• Use visualization, spatial reasoning, and geometric modeling to solve problems.

NCTM Communication Standard for Grades 6–8:

• Organize and consolidate their mathematical thinking through communication;

• Communicate their mathematical thinking coherently and clearly to peers, teachers, and others;

• Analyze and evaluate the mathematical thinking and strategies of others;

• Use the language of mathematics to express mathematical ideas precisely.

NCTM Connections Standard for Grades 6–8:

• Recognize and apply mathematics in contexts outside of mathematics.

Lesson Description

Students will demonstrate their understanding of different types of geometric angles by taking pictures of right, obtuse, and acute angles in the real world. They will send them to Photobucket to store them. Then they will use Photobucket to create a digital storybook that identifies the angles and describes how they would use mathematics to measure them. This activity focuses students on mathematical discourse.

Process

In Class

1. Students learn about geometric angles in class.

2. The teacher asks students to each find three images of different geometric angles (right, obtuse, and acute) in their everyday life outside of school.

3. The teacher sets up a Photobucket account. Here is how:

A. Go to Photobucket at http://photobucket.com.

B. Click on *Join Now*.

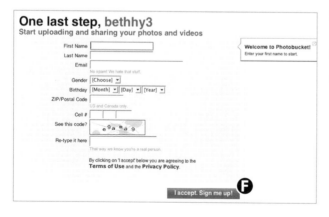

C. Create a username and password (that all your students could use).

D. Click on *Next step*.

E. Complete the sign-up information.

F. Click on *I accept. Sign me up!*

G. You will be brought to your Photobucket account page.

4. The teacher gets the mobile upload address for the students to use. Here is how:

A. Click on *account options*.

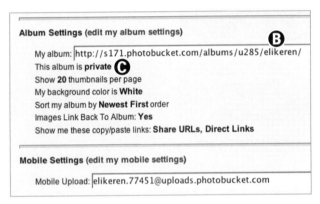

B. In account options, if you scroll down, you will see a mobile upload address. This is what you will give to your students so they can post to the class Photobucket account.

C. Also, you may want to make sure your album is private.

Outside Class

5. For homework, ask your students to take several more pictures of the different types of angles they find in their everyday lives. Students should send the photos to the class Photobucket account using the mobile upload address.

Back in Class

6. Each student should log in to the class Photobucket account. The photos that the students sent should appear in the account.

7. Have students select several pictures from all the photos (not just their own). Then have the students create a slide show. In the slide show, each angle should be labeled. Here is how:

A. Students click on *create remix*.

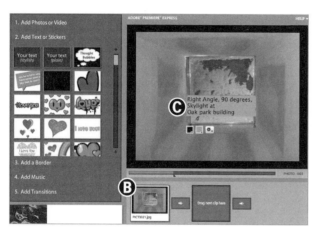

B. In the remix window, students should be able to select from all the student photos in order to put together a slide show remix. First, they should drag their photos into the timeline of the remixer.

C. Next, students should click on *Add Text or Stickers*, and drag a text bubble onto the image (pointing at the specific angle). They should identify the angle in the text bubble.

D. When finished, students should click on *Publish* and provide a title for their slide show.

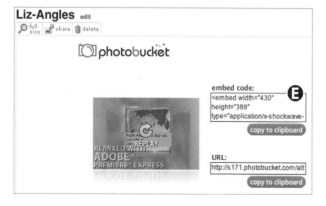

E. Once Photobucket finishes publishing, it will make the slide show available in a window, along with a link where others can view it and code for embedding the slide show into a blog or Web page.

Extensions

- Students can also take pictures of other earth science formations they are studying.

- The teacher could create a class blog or Web site and put pairs of students in charge of creating a Photobucket storybook for each unit they are studying. For example, if students are studying weather and climate, a pair of students could take the pictures and create the Photobucket album. The next month, a different pair of students could be in charge of the new unit on energy.

- Instead of sending pictures, students could send short videos taken with cell phone camcorders to Photobucket.

Lesson Plan 8 ▪ Rock Identification

Content Area	Earth science
Grade Levels	6–9
Tools	Flickr and cell phones
Cost	Free (text-messaging charges may apply)
Standards	NETS•S Performance Indicators for Grades 9–12: 7, 8, 9, 10
	NETS•S Performance Indicators for Grades 6–8: 5, 6, 7, 9
	NSES Standards: Earth and Space Science
	Content Standard D
	◆ As a result of their activities in grades 5–8, all students should develop an understanding of the structure of the earth system

Lesson Description

Often in natural science classrooms, objects are taken out of their natural setting and brought into the classroom to study (such as leaves, soil, or rocks). Students could demonstrate their knowledge of the different natural objects by finding the objects in their natural setting, taking pictures of them with their cell phones, and posting them to the class Flickr site.

Students use their cell phones and Flickr to document and identify different types of rocks they find in their everyday lives. After students document their rock collection, they use the class Flickr account to review the rocks their classmates found.

Process

In Class

1. Each student is given a list of rocks to find for homework.

2. Students are given a tutorial on how to post to the class Flickr account from their cell phones.

3. The teacher sets up a class Flickr account for the students to post to from their cell phones. Here is how:

A. Go to Flickr at http://flickr.com.

B. Click on *Sign Up* to create an account.

C. You will have to sign in through your Yahoo account. If you do not have a Yahoo account, you can sign up for one (there is no cost).

4. Once you create an account, you can set up mobile settings. The teacher sets up the mobile account settings as follows:

A. At your home page, click on uploading *tools*.

B. In Tools, click on *Check out the Flickr Mobile Tools*.

C. In Mobile, click on *upload by email*.

D. You will be given a unique e-mail address where you can send pictures from your cell phone (or any cell phone).

Now your students can take pictures and send them directly to Flickr using this Flickr e-mail address.

5. Give students the e-mail address to use for the class Flickr account.

Outside Class

6. Students go on a "discovery hunt" for the rocks on their list.

7. When they find a rock, they take a picture of it and send it to the class Flickr account with a text message that states what type of rock it is.

Back in Class

8. Using a projector, the teacher logs in to the class Flickr account and asks the students to review the rocks found by their peers. Students should comment on whether their classmates correctly identified the rocks.

Extensions

*   Students can use the Flickr images as "flashcards" to review for an upcoming test or quiz.

*   Students can text the pictures to each other from their cell phones, so that they have the images on their cell phones to review.

*   Students can do the same project with other common natural findings such as insects or leaves.

*   The Flickr images can be transferred to Jumpcut (http://jumpcut.com), which is a free Web 2.0 resource that provides online video-editing similar to Eyespot. At Jumpcut, students can arrange the rock collection images to make a video, then add titles, music, sound effects, video effects, and narration, in a sense creating a "digital rock storybook."

*   In Flickr, students can use the tag feature to label the different minerals found in each rock.

Lesson Plan 9 ▪ PhotoMapping

Content Area	Social studies (geography and history)
Grade Level	6–12
Tools	Flickr and cell phones
Cost	Free (text-messaging charges may apply)
Standards	NETS•S Performance Indicators for Grades 9–12: 7, 8, 9, 10
	NETS•S Performance Indicators for Grades 6–8: 5, 6, 7, 9
	NCSS Standards: I, II, III

Lesson Description

Students will use their cell phones to take pictures of different geographical locations in the local community. They will send their pictures to a class Flickr account, where they will be able to put them on a Flickr map.

Process

In Class

1. The teacher creates a mobile Flickr account (see Lesson Plan 6 for a tutorial on setting up a mobile Flickr account).

2. The teacher gives students the class Flickr e-mail address, so students can send their images directly to the class Flickr account.

3. The teacher asks students to find historical places around town. (Alternatively, students could be asked to find historical sites on their spring break trips.)

Outside Class

4. Students take images of local historical finds and text a short description of their significance. They send their images and descriptions to the class Flickr account.

Back in Class

5. Students log in to the class Flickr account to build their Flickr map. Here is how:

A. Students log in to Flickr at http://flickr.com. They sign in with the class ID and password (the teacher should give this to the students).

B. Students click on the image they took. They should edit the title and description to reflect where the image was taken and the historical significance.

C. Now students click on *Place this photo on a map.*

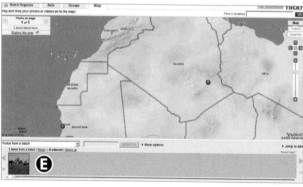

D. The Flickr map will open up. (The teacher can select the default permissions of who can see the images by going to *You, Your Account,* then *Privacy & Permissions.* I recommend selecting *Only You.*)

E. Students can zoom in to the exact location where they took the image and click and drag the image onto the correct location on the map.

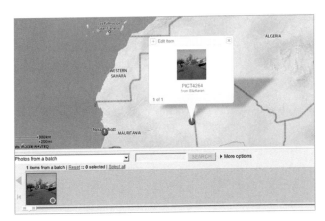

F. The image is now associated with the correct location.

G. Once students have finished, the teacher can open up the map on an LCD projector so everyone can see the map at once. The teacher can open the map by logging in to the class Flickr account and selecting *You,* then *Your Map.*

6. Now the teacher can click on the blue numbered circles to open up each picture and lead a discussion on the geographical region as well as the historical significance of the image.

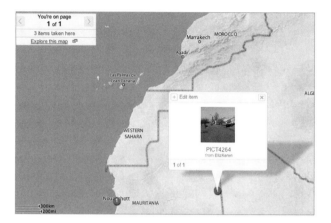

Extensions

- This could be a year-long activity. Students could continue to build a local history map as they encounter different monuments and relics in the community.

- This could also be an assignment for foreign language teachers who are taking their students to a foreign country. The students could take images of different cultural events or experiences, and then map them when they return to the classroom.

- During spring break, students could capture photos of local history in different cities they visit.

- Students could comment on the images of their classmates by using the Flickr comment feature.

Lesson Plan 10 ▪ Geo-Insects

Content Area	Biology/life sciences
Grade Levels	6–9
Tools	Flagr and cell phones
Cost	Free (text-messaging charges may apply)
Standards	NETS•S Performance Indicators for Grades 9–12: 7, 8, 9, 10
	NETS•S Performance Indicators for Grades 6–8: 5, 6, 7, 9
	NSES Standards: Life Science for Grades 5–8
	Content Standard C

Lesson Description

Students will document their understanding of different types of insects by identifying them in their everyday lives, taking pictures with their cell phones, and sending them to a class map on the Internet. With the exact locations pinpointed, the teacher will be able to lead a discussion not only about identifying and categorizing species but also about habitat and ecosystems.

Process

In Class

1. The teacher gives each student a list of insects to find for homework. It is a good idea to give students some time to search for the insects, maybe a week. Spring break is a great time for this assignment.

2. The teacher creates a Flagr account. Here is how:

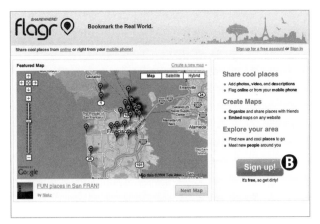

A. Go to Flagr at http://flagr.com.

B. Click on *Sign up!*

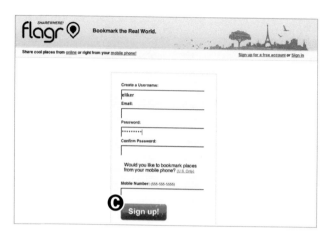

C. Create an account and click on *Sign up!*

3. The teacher creates a class map. Here is how:

A. Log back in to Flagr (if you're not already there).

B. Click on *Invite-Only Map* (this will allow your map to be protected so that only your students can post to it).

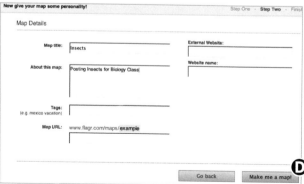

C. Give your map a title, a description, and a name for the URL.

D. Click on *Make me a map!*

4. The teacher extends an invitation to students so that they can post their mobile pictures directly to the class map. Here is how:

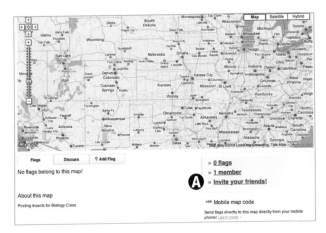

A. Click on *Invite your friends!*

B. Click on *Invite new people.*

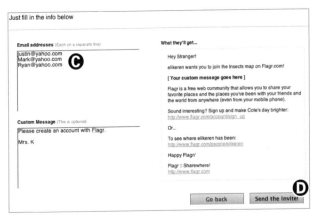

C. Type in the e-mail addresses of your students. (Or create them for your students if they are not allowed to have them. Gaggle is a good resource for creating monitored student e-mail accounts.)

D. Click on *Send the Invite!*

5. Have your students create an account with Flagr so they can post directly to the class map from their cell phones. Your students can create an account at Flagr with their e-mail address. Here is how:

> **A.** Have each student log in to Flagr, click on *Sign up,* and create an account with the same e-mail address that was used when extending the invitations.

6. The teacher gets the mobile e-mail address for the Flagr map. Here is how:

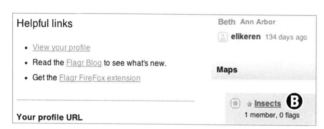

> **A.** Log back in to Flagr at http://flagr.com.
>
> **B.** Click on your "Insects" map (or whatever name you chose) to open it.

> **C.** On the class map, a mobile e-mail address is given in the lower right-hand corner.

7. The teacher gives students the mobile e-mail address. Now students are automatically able to post to the class Flagr map using their cell phone.

8. The teacher explains to students that when they take a picture of an insect, they will send it to the Flagr mobile e-mail address along with a message that indicates the type of insect and where it was found. For example, the message might read "Mosquito@234 Pine road Dexter MI 48108. Found by beth"

Outside Class

9. Students take pictures of insects they find and send them to the class Flagr map.

Back in Class

10. The teacher projects the class Flagr map and discusses each individual photo. Here is how:

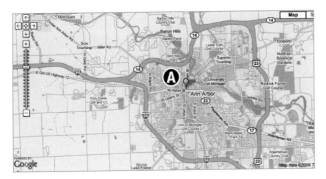

A. The teacher clicks on each flag point in the map to see the insect image. The teacher determines whether each insect is correctly identified. Habitat and ecosystem are also discussed.

Extensions

- The class can use Google Earth to zoom in to see the actual habitat where the insects were found.

- The teacher could make the map public in Flagr and ask people from all around the world to send their images of insects to add to the collection.

- This project could be done with any variety of species found in the local community. It could also be done as a spring break assignment for kids who go outside the community. This provides an opportunity to compare local species with those found at the spring break locale.

Lesson Plan 11 ▪ Telenovela

Content Area	Spanish (or other foreign language)
Grade Levels	9–12
Tools	Eyespot and cell phones
Cost	Free (text-messaging charges may apply)
Standards	NETS•S Performance Indicators for Grades 9–12: 7, 8, 9, 10
	National Standards for Foreign Language Education: 1.1, 1.2, 1.3, 4.1, 4.2, 5.2

Lesson Description

Students in Spanish class will create a short Spanish soap opera (telenovela) using the camcorders on their cell phones. Students will write their script (in Spanish), and then rehearse in class. The students will film for homework, and send their video clips directly from their cell phones to Eyespot for editing. This assignment focuses on both oral and written skills, as well as understanding Spanish culture.

Process

In Class

1. Students are placed in groups of four or five. (Please note that only one student in each group needs to have a cell phone with a camcorder.)

2. To get a sense of what a Spanish telenovela is, students watch clips of telenovelas provided by the teacher.

3. Each group of students writes a script for their own short telenovela. The script should include aspects of Spanish culture that they have learned about or researched.

4. Students get the script approved by the teacher.

5. Students rehearse their scenes in class, so they can get feedback from the teacher on their language skills.

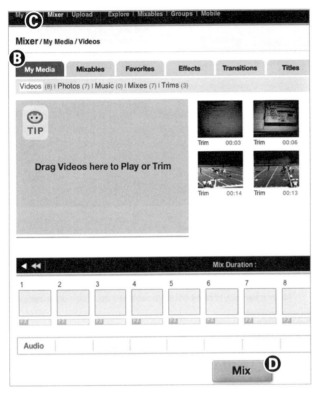

A. Students log in to their Eyespot accounts at http://eyespot.com.

B. In their Eyespot account, students click on *My Media*. The video clips should appear in My Media.

C. Students click on *Mixer* to edit their telenovela.

D. Students export the telenovela by clicking on *Mix*.

E. Students choose options for sharing.

11. Students can download the telenovela or send it to their teacher's e-mail (these are private options). If the goal is to create a published piece of work, students can click on Publish and the telenovela will be published to the Eyespot site.

This will make it visible to the general public. Users will have the option to subscribe to the video feed or embed it on a blog or Web page.

12. Another publication option is to download the video and publish it on TeacherTube (www.teachertube.com), which is similar to YouTube but devoted to teaching and educational videos. (It is a monitored site, and inappropriate videos are reported.) This may be a safer publication option than using the Eyespot general publication site.

Extensions

- Since Eyespot allows users to edit and save videos online, students do not have to be stuck to one computer or a portable hard drive in order to work on their telenovela; they can work on it in school or at home. This allows teachers to spend less class time in the computer lab and more class time on content, while students can edit at home or during study hall.

- Students could have a Foreign Film Festival for the school or parents. They could add subtitles to their telenovelas for anyone who does not speak the language. This would be good practice in written language skills.

- Since many elementary teachers are becoming more interested in starting foreign language learning in early education, advanced language students (11th and 12th graders) can be partnered with elementary classrooms to make introductory foreign language videos for them.

Back in Class

4. The teacher can lead a discussion about the experiences everyone had on their scavenger hunts while viewing the videos in the Eyespot account.

Extension

- This assignment could be done as extra credit for each teaching quarter. For example, the teacher could give out a list of activities during the quarter, such as finding a historical artifact at the local museum or interviewing a chemist. Students could document their items with their cell phones to receive extra credit.

Chapter 5

Developing Classroom Projects for Cell Phones

In this chapter I draw attention to how classroom projects can be developed for cell phones. When students are allowed to create their own learning environments using prior knowledge, they retain more information than in traditional learning environments created by their teachers (Papert, 1980). Educational researchers believe cognitive growth is informed by existing knowledge (Bransford, Brown, & Cooking, 1999; Britton & Graesser, 1996). Classroom activities are more engaging and enriching when students can make connections between a new task and prior knowledge. Because today's students are highly motivated to interact with technology, they may be more motivated to engage in content if they are able to develop content-based projects for their cell phones.

Students are often asked to illustrate their understanding of concepts or ideas by engaging in a creative project such as a skit, a rap, or a collage. We can take this creativity one step further by having students develop these creative projects for their own cell phones, for their parents' cell phones, or even for distribution on multiple cell phones. By publishing these projects to cell phones, students may find them more authentic and engaging, while at the same time learning the classroom content. In addition, the final product will be on their personal cell phones, so they will be constantly reminded of the content they learned, in essence a digital review.

Teachers can make cell phones the focus of classroom projects by asking students to develop unique ringtones, wallpapers, logos, text messages, mobile Web sites, mobile blogs, and mobile surveys and polls. Web 2.0 resources can help make this happen. Furthermore, basic applications such as PowerPoint can be used for mobile presentations. In the next few pages, I describe how to develop these projects and present lesson plans that integrate content and these cell phone features. Once again, cell phones do not have to enter the classroom in order for you to take advantage of these projects.

Ringtones

Phonezoo

Phonezoo (www.phonezoo.com) is a free Web resource that allows users to upload unique ringtones directly to their cell phones. Students can share and publish their ringtones on the Phonezoo site, hence becoming published artists. Phonezoo allows users to upload as ringtones a variety of audio files, such as MP3, WAVE, and MIDI files. Furthermore, Phonezoo gives the option of keeping uploaded ringtones private or publishing them in the Phonezoo directory. When a ringtone is published in the Phonezoo directory, others can use it on their phone. In addition, users can add "friends" in their Phonezoo account so that others can easily listen to and download their ringtones.

Although users cannot create ringtones on the Phonezoo Web site, students can use any audio-editing software to create a ringtone. I recommend Audacity (http://

audacity.sourceforge.net), which is free, easy to use, and compatible with Mac and Windows. If you have a Mac, you could also use GarageBand to create ringtones. In addition, there are many other Web 2.0 resources that will allow free creation, sharing, uploading, and storage of ringtones (see chapter 10 for more examples of ringtone uploading sites). There are many content possibilities for ringtones, such as social studies raps, science jingles, or original poetry. Lesson Plan 13: Math Ringtone Raps or Jingles offers a step-by-step tutorial on using Phonezoo to publish and share ringtones. Lesson Plan 23: Elections also employs Phonezoo.

Wallpaper and Logos

Pix2Fone

Developing wallpapers and logos are also classroom projects for cell phones. Students are often asked to be artistic and illustrate their understanding of concepts and ideas, or express their opinions in a collage or drawing. Normally these images are just posted around the school or classroom. Yet, it may be motivating to students if they could publish their artistic work on cell phones. Not only could they publish on their own cell phones, they could also publish on the phones of their parents, friends, and community members. Using the free Web resource Pix2Fone (www. pix2fone.com), any digital image can become wallpaper on the cell phone.

Students can upload a digital image they created in any paint or drawing program such as Kid Pix or Photoshop, or students can take a picture of a handmade drawing and use it as wallpaper. Pix2Fone includes a basic image editor so that after the image is uploaded to the site, the students can customize the image for the cell phone. In the image editor, students can add speech bubbles, frames, text, and clip art to their pictures. Lesson Plan 14: Travel Postcards offers a step-by-step tutorial on using Pix2Fone. Lesson Plan 23: Elections also integrates the resource. Additionally, chapter 10 provides more examples of Web sites that allow downloading of images to cell phones.

Text Messaging

TextForFree

One of the most popular activities that students do with their cell phones is text messaging. No matter where students are—at the movies, at a ball game, in their bedroom—they love to send and receive text messages. Using Web 2.0 resources, students can send text messages from a computer to any cell phone. This opens up ideas for many classroom projects that can involve the new literacy of text messaging—without having to bring a cell phone into the classroom. A number of Internet resources allow anyone to send a free text message from a computer to a cell phone, and they all work in a similar way. I have selected one of my personal favorites to introduce in this book, TextForFree (http://textforfree.net).

TextForFree (and other text-messaging Web sites) is beneficial because it does not cost anything to send the text messages, whereas if students were sending text messages from their own cell phones, it would often cost a small fee (depending on the plan). Additionally, TextForFree is easy to use. It takes about two minutes to fill out the one-page form and send your text message. Text messages are limited to 140 characters. It is much quicker to send a text message from the computer than to type it into a cell phone. Text messaging can be used for a variety of assignments including advertising, election campaigns, brainstorming, and more. A step-by-step tutorial on using TextForFree is provided in Lesson Plan 15: Who Am I?, an English/language arts activity. Lesson Plan 23: Elections also integrates this resource.

Wiffiti

A common classroom activity is brainstorming sessions, in which the teacher asks students to come up with a variety of ideas on a topic. Or a teacher may ask students a question that could have various answers. While it is common to have students raise their hands and tell their idea (maybe the teacher then writes it on the whiteboard), students can also brainstorm using their cell phones. Taking advantage of another powerful and free Web tool called Wiffiti (http://wiffiti.com), students can immediately send a text message to a live screen online that is updated continuously. The best part of this tool is that students can brainstorm from their cell phones to a live screen on the Web. Since students already text message almost continuously throughout any day, now they can use it for an educational purpose!

Figure 5.1 Joe Wood's science students posting text messages on the class Wiffiti screen

Wiffiti has many fantastic teacher controls such as "approving" messages before they are posted or not allowing content with inappropriate words. You can also keep the screen private or share it with the world. Although I imagine that there are a lot of classroom applications for this tool, one of the best is brainstorming. A teacher who would like students to brainstorm ideas can set up a Wiffiti screen (for free, of course), then tell students (for homework or in class) to text a special code to the general Wiffiti number (25622), along with their brainstorming idea. It will automatically post to the Wiffiti screen that the teacher set up (or the teacher can arrange to approve the messages before they are posted). The screen is live, so this could be done in class at the spur of the moment (if teachers are comfortable with cell phones in the classroom) or for homework so that they have a full brainstorming map before class even begins.

Another nice application of Wiffiti in schools is for observations and notes. For example, if students take a field trip to a local museum, they could text their observations or notes while on the field trip to the class Wiffiti screen, and then back in class they could discuss their experiences. Wiffiti also works with Flickr. The background images on Wiffiti could come from Flickr, and since Flickr has a mobile option, students could also post their images from their field trip to Flickr, and the teacher could select one as the background for the class Wiffiti screen.

Joe Wood is a seventh- and eighth-grade science teacher in California who uses Wiffiti (www.joewoodonline.com). Wood's science students used Wiffiti in an introductory activity to find out what students know about a topic (Figure 5.1). He posed a question to his students, "What do you know about elements, compounds, and mixtures?" The students then text messaged their answers to Wood's Wiffiti account. Wood had the Wiffiti screen projected in the front of the classroom, so his students could view other responses as they messaged.

Lesson Plan 16: Inquiry Question Icebreaker demonstrates a way to use Wiffiti and cell phones for an icebreaker activity. A step-by-step tutorial is included.

Twitter

Currently in Japan mobile novels are popular (see chapter 9). Twitter (http://twitter. com) allows anyone to text message "what they are doing" in 140 characters or less. While it is mostly used as a social resource to keep track of friends' activities, this tool has promise for literary projects.

A new phenomenon has been to create "twittories," or stories written with the assistance of Twitter and cell phones. Since everyone who "follows" you can participate in viewing and writing entries, collaborative story writing becomes a possibility (http:// twittorieswikispaces.com/). For example, one student could start a fiction story, another student could add the next few lines, and so on, until the entire class has contributed to the story. Twitter also allows you to text message online at its Web site, so students who do not have cell phones can still participate in the story development. Furthermore, Twitter offers privacy features such as allowing only invited friends to see your Twitter postings.

Figure 5.2 Barack Obama's official Twitter campaign

Another useful way to use Twitter is for homework help or study groups. Teachers could set up a homework help or study group hotline where students can work together to solve homework problems (because it is on Twitter, teachers can document the thinking process of the students). Teachers could also create a scavenger hunt with Twitter. Students could be assigned homework to find information concerning different topics or concepts in their unit of study. In language arts, for instance, students could try to uncover what certain lines or phrases in a poem might mean or reference. This could even be a game, with students who are first to "twitter" their answers winning the game.

One final note for social studies teachers: Some politicians running for office, such as Barack Obama, have their own Twitter account (http://twitter.com/BarackObama; see Figure 5.2). Students can "follow" various politicians to get a better understanding of their platforms and even communicate with their official campaigns.

Lesson Plan 17: Think-Alouds is a language arts activity that includes a tutorial on using Twitter.

Reactee

Because text messaging is fast becoming a new literacy, coupling it with a popular student item, the graphic T-shirt, creates opportunities for engaging learning projects. Students can develop unique message T-shirts that can "text you back." A Web 2.0 resource called Reactee (http://reactee.com) allows you to create a T-shirt with a personalized slogan and keyword. When others see the T-shirt, they can text in the keyword to their cell phones and receive a personalized message from you. In addition, you can use your cell phone (or the Web site) to update your message as often as you like. Once someone receives your message, they can respond to it.

You can also check the Reactee Web site to see how often people have text messaged your keyword as well as other statistical data. Another feature of Reactee is that people can subscribe to text alerts you send out about the T-shirt topic. For example, if your T-shirt is about global warming, you can send out weekly text alerts about current events related to global warming for anyone who decided to subscribe to the T-shirt. Finally, users can block or filter who can text them back (they can also turn off the text back feature). The shirts can be made public in the Reactee T-Shirt gallery. By putting it in the gallery, people who are purchasing Reactee shirts and like your design could model their shirt after yours. This option might be very motivating to students developing message T-shirts. Although it does cost money to purchase the T-shirts ($20–27, with some discounts), this resource opens up many learning opportunities. Later in this chapter I describe classroom activities that employ Reactee and may prove to be a popular choice among your students. In addition, Lesson Plan 18: Science Activism Project includes a step-by-step tutorial on using Reactee, and Lesson Plan 23: Elections also utilizes this resource.

MobiOde

MobiOde (http://mobiode.com) lets you create free mobile surveys for cell phones that are more complex than a simple instant poll: MobiOde compiles all the statistical information from the survey results. MobiOde creates a unique .mobi Web address for your survey so it is easy to take on any cell phone (or computer). Your students can create a survey or poll for a presentation in order to get feedback after they finish or before they begin. You can send out a poll for the students to complete for homework, so that when they enter class, you will already have a sense of their thoughts on that particular issue. Lesson Plan 21: Scientific Survey provides a step-by-step tutorial on using MobiOde.

Mobile Presentations and Enhanced Podcasts

PowerPoint

Microsoft PowerPoint is probably one of the most common pieces of software used in schools and is also useful for making mobile presentations. This is beneficial for a variety of reasons, one being that students may be more likely to use a PowerPoint presentation to review course material if it is on their always-present cell phone (rather than in a textbook or in written lecture notes). Additionally, students who do not have access to computers at home, but do have access to cell phones, can view and share the PowerPoint presentation through their mobile device.

Students can also create enhanced podcasts with PowerPoint. An enhanced podcast is an audio podcast that includes images or pictures. A good example of enhanced podcasts can be found at the Colonial Williamsburg site History.org (http://history.org/Media/podcasts.cfm). Here, historians have created audio podcasts of different themes from history and included images of particular topics (such as Ben Franklin or a stove from the Revolutionary War era). Students can easily create enhanced podcasts with PowerPoint that can be uploaded to just about any cell phone. Lesson Plan 22: Revolutionary War Enhanced Podcast provides a step-by-step tutorial on creating an enhanced podcast with PowerPoint.

Classroom Ideas

Although it may be enjoyable for students to create ringtones or wallpapers for their cell phones, can we turn these social activities into knowledge-construction projects for the classroom? Perhaps chemistry students, for instance, could turn a popular rap melody into a "periodical chart rap." The following sections provide ways that content-based projects can be built around these hip cell phone applications.

Publishing Poetry

It is important for students to be able to read poetry, recite it, and practice their public speaking. Oral presentations in front of their peers may be difficult and intimidating for some students, and cell phone ringtones provide a nice introduction or alternative to public recitation. Students can recite their own original poetry into an audio editor (such as Audacity or GarageBand) and then send the poetry to their classmates' cell phones using Phonezoo. Additionally, students can make their ringtones public in Phonezoo so others can use their original works as their ringtone. If students are studying popular poets, they can recite the poetry to create ringtones, perhaps inserting a modern drumbeat or melody in the background. Students also could use TextForFree to create 21st-century "poetry messaging," in which they develop poetry for text messaging. They could send their text verses to the cell phones of their friends and family members using TextForFree.

Unit Reviews and Flashcards

Reviewing classroom content can be a rather dull and monotonous activity. Using cell phones, students can create ringtones reviews, or flashcards, of concepts that are being studied in a unit (such as geometric figures). Students can upload classmates' ringtone reviews to their cell phones from Phonezoo, and listen to them to study for an upcoming exam. Most cell phones allow you to assign different ringtones for different cell actions, such as one ringtone for incoming text messages, a different ringtone for incoming phone calls, and yet another for alarms or reminders. Students can assign different flashcard ringtones to specific actions on their cell phones, so that every time their cell phone rings, they can review their content.

Students could use TextForFree to create text-messaging flashcards for each other. In class, students could be placed in groups, where they would be in charge of specific chapter terms. They could create quiz questions or term definitions and text them to students in other groups using TextForFree. Because text messages are saved on cell phones until deleted, students can review for their exams anywhere—

they always have a digital review available. Students could also take advantage of Zinadoo and create mobile Web-site reviews for different units. Once again, they have their built-in study aid on their cell, where they can even review content standing in line for fast food!

Science and Social Studies Jingles and Raps

Science students learn about many difficult subjects such as diseases, life cycles, and elements. Social studies students are required to comprehend equally difficult concepts such as ethnocentrism, democracy, and supply and demand. These studies require memorization of specific details. Science and social studies teachers can turn these occasionally laborious learning exercises into engaging activities by allowing their students to create ringtone jingles or raps. The jingle or rap melody can come from popular music, and students will make up the lyrics to represent the specific information they need to learn. Students can then use ringtones they and their classmates make to review for upcoming exams.

Field Trips and Class Activities

What better way to document class activities than having students create a ringtone of "what they learned" during their field trip? In addition, students can take pictures of their field-trip experiences or class activities and send them as wallpaper to other students' or their parents' cell phones with the help of Pix2Fone. Students can create and publish weekly broadcasts of their activities.

Teachers could use Poll Everywhere to create mobile polls that students could participate in during field trips. Students could "search" for answers to polling questions during the field trip, or they could ask experts at the field trip destination (such as the museum tour guide), then text message their answer to the poll. Another way to document what students are learning on field trips is to have them text message their new knowledge to a Wiffiti board, which can be shared the next class session.

KWLs

Teachers using the KWL technique for a lesson can use Wiffiti as they try to find out what students already know about a topic they are planning to teach. A teacher can ask students to text what they know about the upcoming unit to a Wiffiti board for homework. The next day in class the teacher can lead a discussion on the ideas posted. Poll Everywhere could also be used to find out what students already know. For example, a teacher could set up a poll with a question about an upcoming unit, such as a variety of definitions of gravity. The students could vote using their cell phones on which definition they think is the correct one. The whole class could see the instant voting results on Poll Everywhere (projected in front of the classroom). Then the teacher could ask the students to turn to their neighbor and describe why they voted for their definition. After a few minutes of discussion, the teacher could ask the students to vote again (with their cell phones) to Poll Everywhere to see if anyone's answers had changed as a result of the discussion with their classmate.

1940–1950 Serials

Radio and movie serials were very popular in the mid-20th century. They were made up of short episodes that were broadcast in daily, weekly, or monthly increments (similar to the modern soap opera). A social studies class studying the post-WWII era could develop old-fashioned radio serial ringtones using accurate historical people, events, and settings from the time period. They could develop three or four 30-second episodes for one serial. Each week the students could create and upload a new episode for cell phones (and using Phonezoo, they could have others subscribe to their weekly serial). Likewise, foreign language students could create a telenovela, the Spanish word for a modern-day soap opera, as a radio serial in the language they are studying. This is a great opportunity for students to practice speaking and writing, since they would be writing scripts.

Mobile Business Campaigns

Marketing and advertising are very popular business careers, and a lot of business takes place by cell phone. Teachers of high-school or middle-school business or economics could ask students to develop an entire mobile business campaign for cell phones. Students would first create or choose a product. Next, they would use TextForFree to create advertising slogans for the product and send the slogans to each other. Students could also develop, record, and publish ringtones in the format of a 30-second radio commercial. Students could create their commercials with Audacity, GarageBand, or even Gabcast (see chapter 3) and upload them to cell phones using Phonezoo.

Students could also create an advertising logo for their cell phone wallpaper that could be shared using Pix2Fone. With the assistance of Reactee, students could design message T-shirts to promote their product. When viewers use the T-shirt code, they would get the text-message slogans, the product features, and locations to purchase the product. Finally, students could create a mobile Web site using Zinadoo that advertises the product features and tells where to purchase the product. To make the project more authentic and affordable (text-messaging fees for the picture uploads might be expensive), teachers could ask local businesses to sponsor the project.

Art Galleries and Collages

From paintings to digital images, students at every age level can create their own visual art and display their artwork using the wallpaper feature of Pix2Fone. Students can download each other's artwork to create their own art gallery on their cell phones. In a social studies class, students can create a visual collage that represents the concepts they are studying (such as the American civil rights movement) and upload that as their wallpaper. Students in science class could create data charts or diagrams and upload those to their cell phones as wallpaper. As a result, every time they turn on their cell phone, they have an instant curriculum review.

Mathematical Connections

Mathematics is vital when creating cell phone logos and wallpaper. The images have to be a certain size and proportion in order to look right on the cell phone screen. In addition, cell phones have different screen sizes, so students need to be aware of their cell phone screen size. Therefore, when students create their own wallpaper or logo for their cell phones, they have to figure out the appropriate dimensions for the wallpaper based on their cell phone screen size, and they need a drawing or editing program with access to rules in order to do so. The result should be a perfectly proportioned logo or wallpaper for their cell phone.

In addition, statistical charts and graphs could be uploaded to cell phones as wallpaper for review. Students in a math class can collect survey data by creating a mobile poll with MobiOde or Poll Everywhere and analyze the data with the built-in charts or graphs. They can also practice creating their own graphs of the data.

Current Events

Being aware of current events is a large part of education and lifelong learning. Students in social studies or science courses could use TextForFree to text current events to each other. Individuals or groups of students could be in charge of text messaging current events as they occur in real time. (For example, a social studies student could text message the class when new developments occur in the war in Iraq, or a science student could be in charge of information on stem cell research.) It does not cost students money to send out text messages using a computer, and it would be useful for classmates to have a digital record on their cell phones of the current-event updates. They could use these updates to write a newspaper column or put together a project about their current-event topic. Students could create a T-shirt with Reactee pertaining to a specific current event topic (such as healthcare in the United States), and send out weekly or monthly updates through the Web site. Students could also create a poll to collect and analyze opinions on controversial current events such as views on stem cell research, immigration, or health care. For homework, students could create the poll in Poll Everywhere and ask people to text their answers. Then in class they could present their findings as part of a presentation on the issues or just to start a current-events discussion.

Social Activism and Nonprofit Organizations

Students are often asked to become activists or to support nonprofit charitable organizations. With the assistance of Reactee, students could create T-shirts to promote a social issue of significance to them. For example, students in groups of three or four could design a T-shirt and develop a message about their social topic of choice (e.g., global warming, animal adoption, Darfur, voting rights). The students could change their message once a week (or more or less often), and send out text alerts as new information arises. Furthermore, in the Reactee Web site, students could keep track of the number of people who subscribe to their activism project. Students could also use the T-shirts to raise support by using the message people receive to tell them how to donate their time or money to the cause. To add more authenticity to the project, students could team up with local nonprofits to raise money.

Famous Artists, Academics, and Politicians

Students can use Reactee to design message T-shirts about well-known or up-and-coming artists, authors, mathematicians, scientists, or politicians. The Reactee text message could include a short bio about the chosen person, and people could subscribe to weekly alerts about the happenings or discoveries of that person. For example, if students select a fiction author, they could send text messages about the author's writing, book signings, and facts about the novels. If students select an AIDS researcher, text alerts could include new discoveries or advancements in the researcher's projects. If students select a congressional representative, they could send messages about how the representative is voting or about the bills or committees that the representative is working on.

School Events

Students can use Reactee to design a T-shirt that promotes school and community events. The students can be in charge of sending out text-message alerts to all subscribers about school events such as the spring musical, the jazz band concert, or the Friday night football game. After the events, students could send news briefs about the events such as the final score of the game or a review of the musical or concert. Parents and community members might think it is fun to get periodic updates about school events. Students can also create

7. Once students have recorded their rap or jingle ringtone, they save it as an MP3 file.

8. Now each pair of students sets up a Phonezoo account (where they will be able to send their ringtone to their own cell phones and share them with others). Here is how:

A. Students go to Phonezoo at http://phonezoo.com.

B. Students click on *Sign Up.*

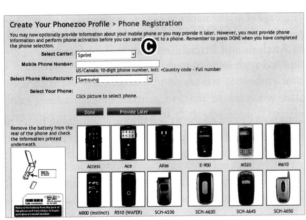

C. Once students sign up, they will be asked to identify their cell phone. Students should put in their cell phone number and carrier then select the brand and type.

9. Now students can upload their ringtone to Phonezoo and then send it to their cell phone. (Remember, they do not have to have their cell phone at school in order to do this project.) Here is how:

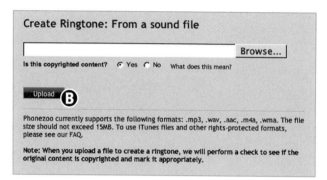

A. Students click on *Create from File.*

B. Students now upload the MP3, WAV, AAC, or MIDI file that was created in GarageBand, Audacity, or other music-editing program.

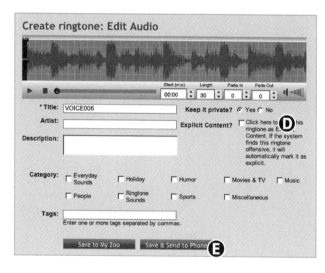

C. After the upload, the ringtone will open up in a new window.

D. Students can adjust the settings (keep it private or make it public), as well as give it a description. If students want to share their ringtone with other students or parents, they can make it public so others can upload it to their cell phones.

E. Now, they click on *Save & Send to Phone.*

Outside Class

10. After school, students can check their cell phone. They should receive a message that their ringtone is in the in-box.

11. Students should open up their ringtone (so it is playing) and store it in their phone.

12. When students wish to change their ringtone settings, their unique ringtone will be available.

13. Students can download their classmates' ringtones from Phonezoo and use them to review the statistical concepts.

Extensions

- Students could take advantage of the Pix2Fone site and upload images that represent the different concepts in the rap or jingle ringtones. This may be beneficial for visual learners.

- Students might do live performances of their raps or jingles in class.

- This assignment could be used for any mathematics or statistics class that focuses on discourse.

- If Phonezoo is not uploading for you, chapter 10 discusses alternative ringtone-uploading resources.

Lesson Plan 14 ▪ Travel Postcards

Content Area	Foreign language
Grade Level	9–12
Tools	Pix2Fone and cell phones
Cost	Free (text-messaging charges may apply)
Standards	NETS•S Performance Indicators for Grades 9–12: 7, 8, 9, 10
	National Standards for Foreign Language Education: 2.1, 2.2, 3.1, 3.2

Lesson Description

Students will create mobile travel postcards that highlight various countries. The postcards will be used as cell phone wallpaper to advertise a trip to a foreign land. In addition, the activity will help students review different aspects of foreign cultures.

Process

In Class

1. Students are given a partner.

2. In pairs, students research different aspects of culture that travelers may want to know about or visit in a foreign country, such as historical landmarks, currency, food, entertainment, cultural norms, and folkways.

3. Using any drawing or paint program (such as Photoshop, Microsoft Paint, AppleWorks, or Microsoft PowerPoint), each pair creates a mobile travel postcard that advertises one aspect of the culture (such as currency).

4. When they finish their postcard, they save it as a JPEG or GIF file.

5. Students send their postcards to their cell phones using Pix2Fone. Here is how:

A. Students log in to Pix2Fone at http://pix2fone.com.

B. Students click on *send now*.

C. Students browse their computer's desktop to find the postcard JPEG or GIF image.

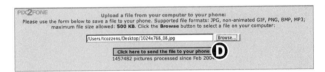

D. Students select *Click here to send the file to your phone.*

E. A new window will open up and ask students to define their cell phone. Students select the brand of cell phone.

F. Now students can adjust their picture to fit their cell phone. They click on *Fit screen* to fit the entire picture into their cell phone screen or, using the blue selection rectangle, they can select the area of the picture they would like to use as their cell phone wallpaper.

G. When finished, students click on *OK* (the red button).

H. A new window will pop up and ask for the cell phone number and cell phone carrier. Students put in the appropriate information and then click on *Send SMS.*

I. A new window will pop up and ask for a verification code (which is sent to the student's cell phone). Students type in the code. The wallpaper will be sent to their phone.

Outside Class

6. Students can send their pictures to each other in order to review the cultural postcards.

Extensions

- Teachers could team up with a travel agency, and the postcards could be used by the travel agency to do mobile travel advertisements. Travel agents might talk to the class and give parameters about what to include and not include in the wallpaper advertisements.

- Instead of travel postcards, students could create image collages that represent multiple aspects of the culture (rather than just one topic per postcard).

- Students can create 30-second sound advertisements for traveling to the country (integrating authentic music along with their oral language skills). Using Phonezoo, students could upload these to their cell phones as ringtones and share them with their classmates as part of the mobile travel campaign. When the students' cell phone rings, they will have wallpaper and a ringtone that helps them review their cultural knowledge of a specific foreign country.

- If Pix2Fone is not uploading for you, chapter 10 discusses alternative image-uploading resources.

Lesson Plan 15 ▪ Who Am I?

Content Area	English/language arts
Grade Level	6–12
Tools	TextForFree and cell phones
Cost	Free
Standards	NETS•S Performance Indicators for Grades 6–8: 7, 8, 9, 10
	NETS•S Performance Indicators for Grades 9–12: 7, 8, 9, 10
	NCTE Standards: 3, 4, 8

Lesson Description

Students will create "Who am I?" character text messages to demonstrate their understanding of characters in novels. The text messages will assist students and their classmates in reviewing their class readings.

Process

In Class

1. Students are paired up.

2. Each pair of students is assigned a character from the novel the class is reading (e.g., Holden Caulfield from *Catcher in the Rye*, or the Friar from *Canterbury Tales*).

3. Students take some time to figure out what defines their character. The teacher may even give students a list of characteristics they should consider for their character. (For example: If the character were alive today, where would he or she live? What type of food would he or she enjoy? What would the character's favorite movie be and why?)

4. Students develop two or three text messages giving clues to the character but not telling who the character is. For example: "I like money more than my friends"; "I own many businesses"; or "I'll never get married."

5. Students in each group send their text messages to students in other groups using TextForFree. Here is how:

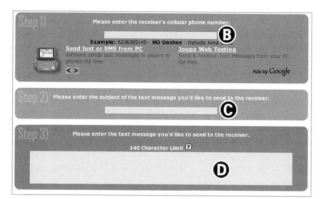

A. Students log in to TextForFree at http://textforfree.net.

B. Students type in the phone number they want to send the text message to.

C. Students type in the topic of their message.

D. Students type in the body of their message (no more than 140 characters).

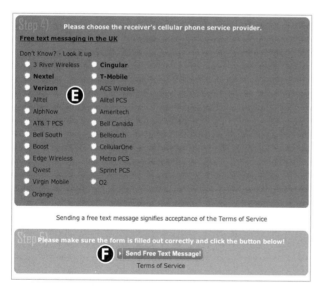

E. Students select the service provider of the receiver's phone

F. Students select *Send Free Text Message!*

Outside Class

6. Students check their new text messages on their cell phones to try to solve the "Who am I?" mystery. This exercise will help them review the character connections in the novel. Students now have a digital review.

Extensions

- To help motivate students, the teacher could have prizes for students who solve the "Who am I" mysteries first. To give the answers, students must use their cell phones or a computer to submit their answers via text message or e-mail their teacher. The teacher will know the order that the messages come in by their time stamps. It may create a mad dash to student cell phones right after school, but isn't it better to see students want to use the cell phone for a learning purpose rather than simply for socializing?

- This activity could be used for a concept or vocabulary review.

- Students could be in charge of different aspects of a new novel, such as setting, plot, characters, location, and author. They could send out quick text messages to their peers summarizing the basics of the novel.

Lesson Plan 16 ▪ Inquiry Question Icebreaker

Content Area	Any
Grade Level	6–12
Tools	Wiffiti and cell phones
Cost	Free (text-messaging charges may apply)
Standards	NETS•S Performance Indicators for Grades 6–8: 7, 8, 9, 10
	NETS•S Performance Indicators for Grades 9–12: 7, 8, 9, 10

Lesson Description

Students will use their cell phones to post possible answers to an inquiry question posed by the teacher. The students' cell phone text-message answers will immediately post to a live screen hosted by Wiffiti. This lesson can be used as an introduction to any unit.

Process

In Class

1. Before starting a new unit, the teacher will create a class account in Wiffiti. Here is how:

A. Go to Wiffiti at http://wiffiti.com.

B. Click on *Sign Up.*

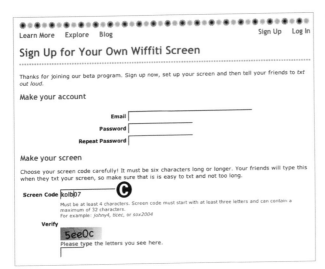

C. Create your account and pay special attention to the screen code, because this is what your students will have to text message to when they send a message to the class Wiffiti screen.

D. Once you create your screen, Wiffiti will tell you to text @yourscreencode to the general Wiffiti number, which is 25622.

2. Using your own cell phone, show students how to text their messages to the Wiffiti board. Remind them to send their message to 25622, and in the actual message prompt they should text @thescreencode and then their message. Their message should look like this on their cell phones: *@Kolb07 slavery is a cause of CW*

3. You may want to practice in front of the students so they see how to text to the screen with their cell phone.

Outside Class

4. For homework, students post their possible answers to the inquiry question. You may want to assign them a reading activity to give them ideas or ask them to question people they know.

Back in Class

5. The teacher logs in to the class Wiffiti screen.

6. The class discusses the potential answers to the inquiry question.

Extensions

- The teacher can have students post images that represent their answer on Flickr. The student with the image that best represents the answer will have his or her image posted as the background for the class Wiffiti screen.

- If teachers are comfortable, they can do this activity instantly in-class by having their students use their cell phones to text ideas to the board. The discussion screen will change "live" in front of the students.

- Teachers can also change the Wiffiti settings under Messages to moderate all posts before they are sent to the board, in case there is a fear of inappropriate posts.

- Teachers can return to the Wiffiti screen at the end of the unit to see if students' answers to the inquiry question have been modified as a result of the teaching and learning during the unit.

- Instead of only students coming up with the text-message answers, they could ask friends and family to text message in their answers too!

Lesson Plan 17 ▪ Think-Alouds

Content Area	Language arts
Grade Level	6–12
Tools	Twitter and cell phones
Cost	Free (text-messaging charges may apply)
Standards	NETS•S Performance Indicators for Grades 6–8: 7, 8, 9, 10
	NETS•S Performance Indicators for Grades 9–12: 7, 8, 9, 10
	NCTE Standards: 3, 4, 8

Lesson Description

For homework, students will use Twitter to post their reading reactions (think-alouds) to the class novel. This will help the teacher prepare for the discussion the following day in class.

Process

In Class

    1. The teacher asks each student to create a Twitter account. Here is how:

    A. Students go to Twitter at http://twitter.com.

    B. Students click on *Get Started—Join!*

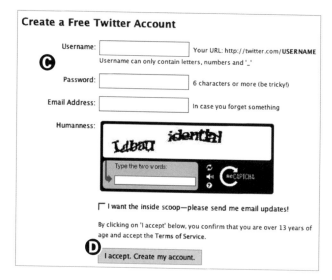

C. Students fill out the form to create their accounts and then give the teacher their username and password. (Teachers could also create the accounts for students so teachers would always have control over the accounts.) If students are not allowed to use e-mail in school, the teacher may want to register students for filtered e-mail service at Gaggle (http://gaggle.net).

D. Students should click on *I accept. Create my account.*

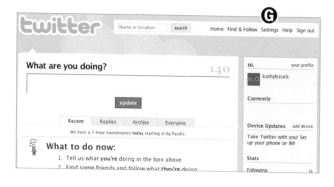

E. Students will now be asked to type in their e-mail to see if they have any friends on Twitter. They can click on *continue* to create their account.

F. Now students are in their home page window.

G. Once students have created their accounts, they can click on *Settings* and then *Devices* to set up their mobile phone numbers.

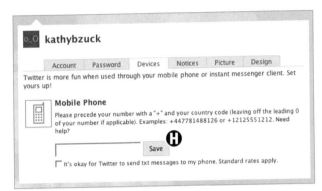

H. Students should enter their cell phone number and click on *Save.*

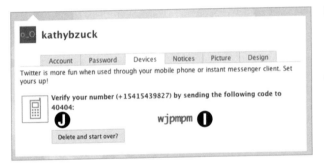

I. Now students will get a message telling them to text a code to Twitter to complete setup of their mobile account.

J. Once students have completed the text message to Twitter, they can text to the Twitter number (40404) at any time and it will directly post to their Twitter account.

2. The teacher should also set up a Twitter account.

3. Students can now share their accounts with each other and their teacher. Here is how:

A. Students log in to their Twitter accounts.

B. Once students are in their accounts, they can go to the *search* field and type in their teacher's Twitter ID (the teacher should give this to students). Alternatively, students can click on *Find & Follow.*

C. Once they find their teacher's account, they click on the *follow* button. They will automatically start to receive updates from their teacher, and their teacher now has access to the student "follower" accounts.

Outside Class

4. For homework, students read their assignment in the class novel and then use their cell phones to post their reactions to Twitter by text messaging to 40404. (If they do not have cell phones, they could use instant messaging on the Internet.)

5. The teacher will get instant updates in the Twitter account. (Teachers can also sign up through Twitter to receive them on their cell phone.)

6. If students choose to "follow" other students, they will get updates of their classmates' reactions. They can respond to them through their cell phone by text messaging a reply to 40404.

7. If every student subscribes to the teacher's Twitter account, they will see all of their classmates' think-alouds in the teacher's account. (The students and the teacher do not have to check every Twitter account; they can go to just the teacher's account and view all the responses.)

Back in Class

8. The teacher leads a discussion on the reaction think-alouds.

Extensions

- Students can post review questions on Twitter for each other about different happenings in the novel. For example, a student can text, "What is the historical time period in which this novel takes place?" Other students can text their replies. Since Twitter records the entire text conversation, students will have a nice review document when they are finished with their questions.

- The teacher could spontaneously send out Twitter text-message review questions for students to answer. There could even be prizes or extra credit for students who answer the questions first.

- The teacher can also set up more protection for the Twitter accounts by having the students click on Settings, then Account, and then Protect my Updates. This way only invited followers can see the Twitter messages on the accounts.

Lesson Plan 18 ▪ Science Activism Project

Content Area	Science
Grade Level	9–12
Tools	Reactee and cell phones
Cost	Yes. The T-shirts cost $20–27 per shirt (discounts are available)
Standards	NETS•S Performance Indicators for Grades 9–12: 7, 8, 9, 10

NSES Standards: History and Nature of Science

Content Standard G: As a result of activities in grades 9–12, all students should develop understanding of

+ Science as a human endeavor
+ Nature of scientific knowledge
+ Historical perspectives

Lesson Description

At the beginning of the term, students will be placed in groups and become experts on a historically significant scientific phenomenon such as germ theory, nuclear physics, atomic theory, biological evolution, or plate tectonics. Students will find modern-day links to these perspectives (such as global warming and plate tectonics) in order to understand how these theories are evolving over time. Then, students will create a Reactee T-shirt design to represent the connection between past and present phenomena. They will devise a text message to let people know about the connection and how it affects society today. Students will provide weekly or monthly text-message alerts to all subscribers of their Reactee T-shirts with updates on additional connections they discover.

Process

In Class

1. Students are placed in groups of three.

2. Students research a historically significant scientific phenomenon.

3. Students research modern-day connections to the phenomenon and learn how it affects society today.

4. Students design a Reactee T-shirt. Here is how:

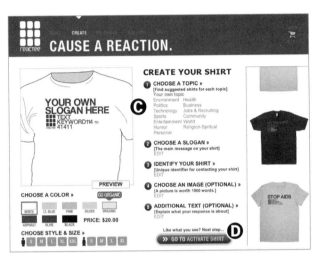

A. Students go to Reactee at http://reactee.com.

B. Students click on *CREATE YOUR OWN SHIRT!*

C. Students select their options—slogan, keyword for text message, and image. They can even upload their own image.

D. After they select their options, students click on *GO TO ACTIVATE SHIRT.*

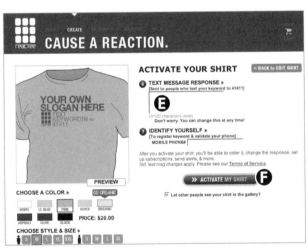

E. At the Activate Your Shirt window, students type in the text message response that people will receive when they text the shirt code. The text message should be informative about their chosen topic. They must also provide identifying information.

F. Now students can click on *ACTIVATE MY SHIRT.*

Outside Class

5. Once the shirts are delivered, students can sell them or wear them to try to elicit subscribers.

6. Every week or month, students can update the text message or send out a new alert to subscribers about current updates on their issue.

Back in Class

7. Students can check the Reactee site for statistics on how many subscribers they have to their alert and how many have text messaged their keyword.

Extensions

- The teacher could make this project into more of a competition to see how many subscribers each group can get. The winning team receives an educational prize.

- Students could create an informational blog or Web site on their topic and use the text-message feature of Reactee to point subscribers to their blog or Web site.

- Students could partner up with a local nonprofit science organization to raise awareness about the organization's goals and to garner donations.

Lesson Plan 19 ▪ Stay Healthy!

Content Area	Science or health education
Grade Level	9–12
Tools	Zinadoo and cell phones
Cost	Free
Standards	NETS•S Performance Indicators for Grades 9–12: 7, 8, 9, 10

National Health Education Standards:
  - NPH-H.9–12.3 Reducing Health Risks
  - NPH-H.9–12.5 Using Communication Skills to Promote Health
  - NPH-H.9–12.2 Health Information, Products, and Services

Lesson Description

Students will create a mobile-friendly Web site regarding nutrition and fitness. The mobile Web site will allow users to have a diet and nutrition resource with them at all times. It will even include ways to document their daily exercise.

Process

In Class

1. Students conduct research on nutrition, diet, and exercise.

2. Students find Internet resources that will help them do the following:

   - Keep track of their daily nutrition

   - Keep track of their daily exercise

   - Give them tips on staying healthy

   - Discuss current issues in health education

3. Students create a mobile-friendly Web site with Zinadoo that integrates all of their health education research. Here is how:

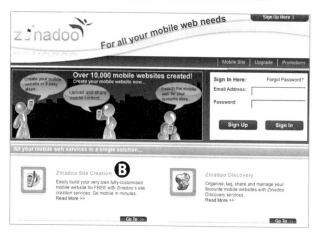

A. Students go to Zinadoo at http://zinadoo.com.

B. Students click on *Zinadoo site creation.*

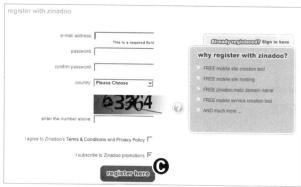

C. Students enter the correct information to create the Zinadoo account. They then click *register here.*

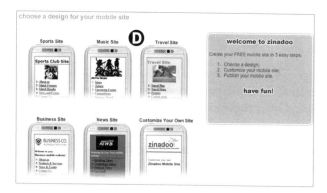

D. Now students can select their mobile Web site template (just like selecting a background in PowerPoint or Publisher).

E. Once they have chosen their background, students can adjust their mobile Web site by adding text, links (to health education sites), images, and other media. They can also preview it in the preview phone window.

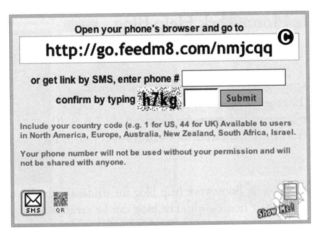

C. You will be given an SMS link to send directly to your cell phone.

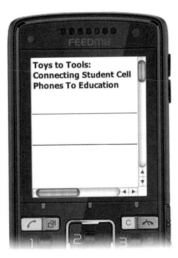

D. You will get a preview of your mobile blog and posting options.

3. Give your students the mobile Web address, so that if they want to reference math help at any time, they can simply look on their cell phone.

Extensions

- Students could be in charge of updating the homework help blog.

- Instead of creating just a homework help blog, teachers could expand on the idea and add other features to the blog, such as a class calendar, student projects, class news, and even resources.

- Instead of making a new blog, the teacher or students could turn a favorite educational blog into a mobile blog. For example, a CNN blog could become mobile using FeedM8.

- Students can also sign up for mobile text alerts through FeedM8, so they would know instantly when the teacher has posted more information on the homework help blog.

Lesson Plan 21 ▪ Scientific Survey

Content Area   Science
Grade Level   9–12
Tools   MobiOde, Excel, and cell phones
Cost   Free (mobile Internet charges may apply)
Standards   NETS•S Performance Indicators for Grades 6–8: 7, 8, 9, 10
    NETS•S Performance Indicators for Grades 9–12: 7, 8, 9, 10
    NSES Standards
        Content Standard A: As a result of activities in grades 9–12,
        all students should develop
        ◆ Abilities necessary to do scientific inquiry
        ◆ Understandings about scientific inquiry

Lesson Description

Students will use MobiOde to develop a survey with an inquiry question about a scientific phenomenon (such as "What is global warming?"). They will use their survey results to create a data chart in Microsoft Excel.

Process

In Class

1. Students decide on their science topic and the question they will ask in their survey.

2. Students create a MobiOde account and write their survey. Here is how:

   A. Students go to MobiOde at http://mobiode.com.

   B. Students click on *Sign up.*

   C. Students are asked to fill out a form with their login name, password, real name, and e-mail address.

D. Once the account has been created, students will create their survey.

E. Students click on *Surveys*.

F. Students select *Create new survey*.

G. Students should create the descriptions for their survey and then click on *Create new survey*.

Create survey

Survey name: Global Warming   Name of your survey.

Domain name: Global   Unique identifier under survey will be acsesib word.

Welcome text: Welcome to the Period 1 Global Warming Survey!   This text will be display

Thank you text: Thank you for taking the survey. Visit our website for results later this month.   This text will be display

URL to your logo or picture: URL adress to a picture

Back URL: URL adress to your mok should start with http://

Survey language: English   Language of your survey

Create new survey (G)

H. Now students are given their domain name. It should have a .mobi at the end, which means that the survey is "mobile ready." It can be accessed and taken on a cell phone with Internet access.

I. Students should click on *create the first question* for your survey.

J. Students should create Question 1 (they have a choice of multiple choice or fill-in-the-blank).

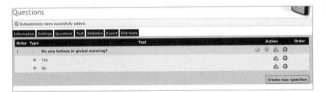

K. Now students should create options (which are the possible answers) for their question. They can have as many options as they want.

L. When students are done creating their options, they can click on *Create and end*.

M. A window will open with the survey question and options.

N. Now students click on *Information*.

O. Students select *Launch the survey*.

3. Students send out their MobiOde mobile survey link to their classmates (or anyone they would like to take the survey). The survey can be taken on a cell phone or on a computer (just in case some of the participants do not have Internet access on their cell phones).

Outside Class

4. Participants will take the survey (using a cell phone or computer).

Back in Class

5. Students log in to MobiOde and collect their data results in an Excel spreadsheet. Here is how:

A. Students log in to MobiOde at http://mobiode.com

B. They click on *Surveys*.

C. Now students click on *Statistics* for their survey.

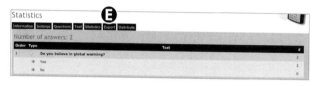

D. Students can view the statistics in the window.

E. To send the data to Excel, students should click on *Export*.

F. Once they click on the *Export* link, the data should automatically open as a new spreadsheet in Excel.

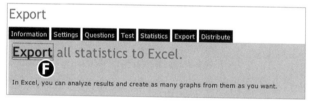

G. The spreadsheet should look like this.

Extensions

- Students could save their Excel spreadsheet data as a chart or graph, which they could upload to cell phones as a picture (by using http://cellfish.com).

- Instead of using MobiOde, students could use Poll Everywhere (http://polleverywhere.com), which would allow them to see instant results in a live graph.

Lesson Plan 22 ▪ Revolutionary War Enhanced Podcast

Content Area	Social studies
Grade Level	6–12
Tools	PowerPoint, QuickTime Pro, Mobilatory, and cell phones
Cost	Free (text-messaging charges may apply)
Standards	NETS•S Performance Indicators for Grades 6–8: 7, 8, 9, 10
	NETS•S Performance Indicators for Grades 9–12: 7, 8, 9, 10
	NCSS Standards: I

Lesson Description

Students will use PowerPoint to create enhanced mobile podcasts concerning everyday life in the Revolutionary War era. Topics may include clothing, entertainment, heating, shelter, transportation, or cooking. Students will each create a 30-second presentation on a different topic and then upload it to their cell phones. Students can use the podcasts for quick review using their mobile phones.

Process

In Class

1. The teacher describes enhanced history podcasts and shows examples, available at History.org (http://history.org/Media/podcasts.cfm).

2. Students research their chosen topic of everyday life in colonial times.

3. Students open up PowerPoint and create a new presentation. Here is how:

A. Students create their first slide.

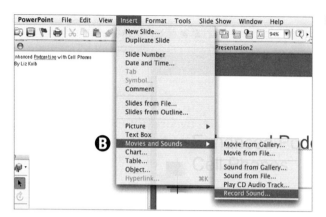

B. Students record the narrative to go with the first slide. To do this, they go to *Insert > Movies and Sounds > Record Sound*.

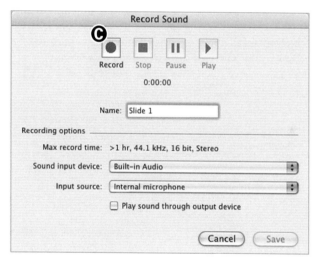

C. A sound recorder will appear. When they are ready, students click on *Record* (the red button) and record their narration. When they are done, they click on *Save*.

D. Students should continue to create as many slides as they need in their presentation.

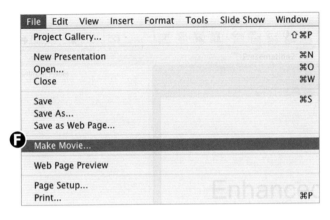

E. Once they are finished with their presentation, they can make a movie with PowerPoint:

F. Go to *File > Make Movie.*

G. When the save menu appears, students should select to save the movie to the desktop.

H. The PowerPoint movie is saved in QuickTime format (.mov). It can be opened using QuickTime Pro or a free online converter.

I. Students can now close PowerPoint.

4. Now students need to send their enhanced podcast to their (and their classmates') cell phones. To do this, they will need to convert their PowerPoint movie to the 3G format (movies can be viewed on a cell phone only in the 3G format). Here is how:

A. On the desktop, students should double-click on the PowerPoint movie icon that they just created to open it up (it should open in QuickTime Pro).

If QuickTime Pro is not available, students can use a free online converter such as Zamzar (http://zamzar.com) or Media-Convert (http://media-convert.com).

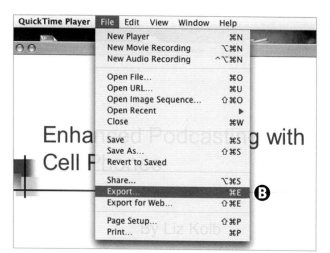

B. In QuickTime Pro, students go to *File > Export > Movie to 3G*

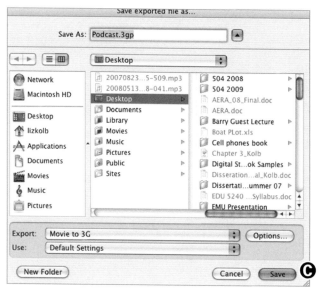

C. Students select Save.

D. The enhanced podcast for their cell phone is now complete.

E. Once the 3G file is on the desktop, students can upload it to the video message sender at Mobilatory (www. mobilatory/com/send/).

Other mobile uploading tools include Cellfish (http://cellfish. com) and txt60 (http://txt60. com).

F. In Mobilatory, students click on *Browse* to find their converted movie file.

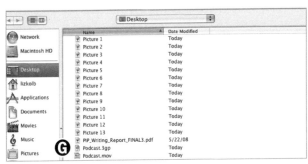

G. Students browse to find their 3G file on the desktop.

H. Now students select the mobile operator, enter the mobile phone number, and click on *Send to phone.*

Outside Class

5. Students should receive a new message on their cell phone with their enhanced podcast in about 10 minutes (depending on the size of the file).

6. They can also send their enhanced podcasts to their classmates' cell phones once it is on their own.

7. They can now access their mobile-enhanced podcasts at their convenience to review for an upcoming test.

Extension

- Students can also create enhanced podcasts for the iPod in iTunes using the QuickTime Pro iPod export option.

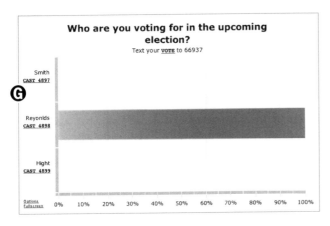

G. Once students select Open Poll, the text numbers for each option appear.

H. Students can e-mail the text numbers for each option or simply hand out a flier with the numbers on it.

Outside Class

6. Students use their mobile devices to "get the word out" about their candidate and try to register voters. Students use their T-shirt to help register voters.

7. Students try to get 100 people to text message their vote to the poll.

8. The group that registers the most voters will win the class election. The students can keep track of how many have registered to vote with the statistics posted by Reactee.

Back in Class

9. The class discusses how effective mobile campaigning was for them and for their candidates.

10. The class discusses the results of each group's mobile poll. The teacher announces the winner.

Extensions

- Students can create a stump speech using Gabcast (see chapter 3).

- Students can create a Web page or blog about their candidate.

- Students can focus even more on the next generation of voters by using their social-networking skills to stump for a candidate (such as developing a MySpace site for the candidate). They could also create an enhanced podcast.

- The teacher could have students visit the local campaign office of the candidate of their choice and ask how they can help.

- The students could contact the local campaign office of their candidate and find out if they can develop mobile campaigns for the candidate's Web site.

- Students could create a 30-second campaign advertisement for TV using Eyespot and camera cell phones (see chapter 4).

Chapter 6

Cell Phones as Research and Organizational Tools

It is important for students to have opportunities to conduct research outside of school in real-world settings. Yet in natural settings, students do not have access to the tools (scientific calculators, research journals, or data-entry software) they need to successfully collect data and organize their research. In addition, students often have trouble managing their school assignments, and need a convenient way to organize their lives. Cell phones have the potential to become practical and accessible research and organizational tools for students.

Most cell phones allow access to the Internet, where one can surf a variety of resources. Currently mobile Internet surfing is a bit awkward. It can be slow and difficult to navigate certain sites. Furthermore, some cell phone providers charge extra for Web surfing. In the next few years, however, Web browsing with cell phones will be easier and Internet access will likely be a basic part of cell phone service. Therefore, it is important to consider how Web browsing on cell phones can benefit education. Even basic cell phones have many built-in research and organizational tools, such as a calendars or date books, voice recording, and calculators. These mobile features can be utilized a variety of ways to aid in education. This chapter describes how cell phones can be valuable tools for research and organization.

The Benefits of Web Surfing by Cell Phone

Although it is easier to surf the Internet on a computer (larger keyboard, larger screen), we do not yet have wireless access to the Internet everywhere. In addition, most students do not have their own mobile computers, especially in lower income areas. Because many cell phones can connect to the Internet, they can be important and valuable research tools in the real world. Additionally, cell phones with Internet access may be an equalizer in the digital divide for students who do not have computers at home. One explanation given by teachers who are not using Internet resources with their students is that they do not want to assign Web-based homework or research because not all their students have computers or Internet access at home. Cell phones may fill in the gap here. Statistically, economic status does not seem to be a factor in ownership of cell phones among students.

If teachers would like their students to participate in a class wiki or in a weekly online discussion, it may be difficult to reserve the computer lab or mobile laptops every week, and taking valuable class time to complete the activity may not be a viable option. By taking advantage of the Internet capabilities of student cell phones, teachers can assign online activity for homework without digital equity worries. Students can also view the school and class Web sites to receive valuable information. In addition, Internet access on cell phones allows students to access information when they are participating in school-sponsored activities outside the classroom. For example, if on a class field trip to the art museum, teachers wanted their students to research the work of an unfamiliar artist while looking at an original piece of art, students would access an online encyclopedia using their cell phones, and learn about the artist at that particular moment. They could even immediately create a podcast (see chapter 3) or photoblog (see chapter 4) about the artist before they leave the art museum.

Web Site Access

Although not all Web sites currently are "cell phone friendly" (easy to surf and interact with on a mobile device) many popular reference Web sites are. For example, Google (www.google.com/mobile/) and Yahoo (http://mobile.yahoo.com) have mobile-friendly Internet searching. Additionally, most e-mail hosts such as Yahoo and Gmail allow you to access your e-mail with your cell phone. Numerous online encyclopedias and reference sites such as Wikipedia are cell phone friendly. Web sites that are cell phone friendly often have a special Web site address known as .mobi, or dotMobi. Wikipedia has a .mobi site called Wapedia. Wapedia allows anyone to easily surf all articles of Wikipedia through a cell phone. Teachers or students can type in http://wapedia.mobi/en/ to their cell phone Internet browser. This provides instant access to Wikipedia.

Chapter 9 discusses the future of cell phones. Experts predict that most Web sites will soon become cell phone friendly. This will open up more learning opportunities for students outside the classroom, and more opportunities for students to connect their classroom learning tool, the cell phone, with their everyday culture. To find out if a Web site is mobile friendly, go to ready.mobi (http://mr.dev.mobi/). When you get to the ready.mobi Web site, just type in any Web address to see how well it can be viewed on a cell phone. By checking a site to see if it is mobile friendly, teachers can plan ahead for student homework assignments. Chapter 5 addresses how students can create their own mobile-friendly Web sites as classroom projects.

Classroom Web Sites and Educational Resources

Many Web resources permit teachers to create Web sites that contain information on assignments and other pertinent classroom details. One site in particular, called HomeworkNOW (http://homeworknow.com), allows parents and students to access school information using their cell phones. Because more students (and

organizational tool in school, students learn how to use their cell phone as a lifelong professional resource.

Calculators

Most cell phones are equipped with a basic calculator. Calculators are often used in mathematic and science classrooms. Some school districts purchase classroom sets of calculators for students to use. Often, school policies prohibit students from removing their school calculators from the classroom, limiting their use to when they are in school. At the secondary level, students invest in expensive graphing calculators to complete their mathematic and science assignments. While most cell phone calculators do not have complex equation editors or graphing features, this is likely to change in the near future. As a result, students will no longer need to purchase a separate calculator for their class assignments and projects. This means that when students are outside of school, they will have access to their calculation tools, anytime, anywhere. Ready access means more real-world homework assignments. For example, students studying measurement systems can use their cell phones to calculate the "best bargains" of the same item in different size packaging in a grocery store. Students can even use the camera to take pictures of the items, or use the voice-recording feature to note their mathematical observations. Once again, the social toy is turned into a useful educational tool.

Chapter 7

Cell Phones as Management Tools

Cell phones have great potential for classroom learning connections, but they can also be effective management tools for everyday tasks. Teachers are always looking for better ways to get to know each of their students, to evaluate collaborative groups, to manage students effectively during extracurricular activities, to help keep them safe, to stay in touch with parents, and to manage students who miss class sessions. This chapter illustrates how cell phones can help teachers manage their students and classroom activities.

Student Supervision

Teachers look for ways to better know each student's individual interests and abilities, but often do not have time during the school day to connect with every student. Since most students have their own cell phone with them at all times, teachers can take advantage of the portable communication tool to better connect to them. For example, teachers can conduct conferences with their students by cell phone. The conferences can be to check in on a big project or simply to make sure they are mentally well. Normally these types of check-in conferences are conducted during school hours, since reaching students after hours is inconvenient. Now that so many students have their own cell phone, teachers can save class time and have more one-to-one contact time with their students by conducting the conferences before or after school hours.

Using FreeConferencePro (see chapter 3), teachers can record a conference and save it in private space at the Web site so they have documentation of the discussion. Teachers can also use FreeConferencePro to have parents call in for the conference (this is helpful if parents are divorced or not able to be at the same phone as the students). Again, the call can be documented so the teacher has a record of what has occurred.

Group Activities

Two of the most difficult aspects of conducting collaborative group activities in the classroom are assessing individual contributions and making sure groups stay on task. Currently teachers often have to venture from group to group, listening in on conversations, and require students to complete evaluations to document what and how they contributed to the project. None of these methods, however, gives the teacher total access to the group's brainstorming or activities. Using Gabcast and a student cell phone, teachers can have their students record the group's brainstorming, discussions, and other activities live. The students can post the recording to Gabcast's private space, and the teacher can log in at a convenient time to monitor the progress. In addition, if some group meetings occur outside of school, students can still record and document the progress.

Although a tape recorder can be used to do the exact same thing, you would need at least six to ten tape recorders to monitor every class group. Students actually remembering to bring the tape recorder and the tape actually working are other concerns with this method. Students hardly ever forget to bring their cell phones with them, no matter where they go. In addition, teachers may appreciate being able to download the MP3 audio files from Gabcast to their MP3 player or a CD so they can listen "on the go" rather than being stuck at a table with a tape recorder and a couple dozen audio tapes. Also, if students know that they are being recorded during their group discussions, they may be more likely to stay on task and be more productive (as opposed to being productive only when the teacher is sitting in on their group discussion).

Field Trips and Extracurricular Events

Extracurricular activities can be difficult for teachers to manage. Often this is because students have more freedom during these activities. For example, in an after-school journalism club, students may be permitted to venture out into the community to report on stories or look for sponsorship. It is tricky for the teacher to keep track of the students and make sure they are on task and safe. The same is true for field trips. At the middle-school level, parent volunteers often help chaperone field trips, where they may be in charge of small groups of four to five students, and the students often have permission to explore away from the teacher. Teachers are still responsible for the students during the field trips and need to be available for parent questions, problems, or issues. Additionally, high school students are often allowed to venture off in their own groups on field trips. Cell phones can be effective tools for monitoring students and parent volunteers. Furthermore, cell phones can be a safety tool for students if they are involved in a troubling situation during the field trip.

While students can use their cell phones to conduct interviews or store images of their field trip or extracurricular experience, the teacher can use cell phones to call, text message, and check in on the students and parents. At the end of the field trip, the teacher can send out an alert from his or her cell phone to remind students and parents to return to the bus or an appropriate meeting spot. Teachers can take advantage of being able to retrieve immediate voice-mail messages with a YouMail account (see chapter 3). Teachers can make sure that students are completing their assignments during the field trip (such as conducting an interview or recording verbal observations) by dialing in to the YouMail voice mail to listen to which students have completed their assignments. If students are not doing their interviews or verbal assignments properly, or if they have questions, the teacher can give them immediate feedback and help by cell phone.

Jott is also a useful management tool. Using cell phones, students can easily dictate research notes, data collection, or brainstorming ideas using Jott's speech-to-text feature (see chapter 3). Those notes can be immediately stored in student Jott accounts and sent to them by e-mail. Students can also send the information directly to their teachers by e-mailing them or CC'ing them in their Jott accounts. This allows teachers to check the progress of students and manage their learning. Students can then return to class (without needing a cell phone) and open up their Jott account online to download or listen to their notes.

Student Safety

In a time when we have many concerns over student safety, cell phones can be helpful in keeping students protected before and after school. Safety is one of the biggest reasons why some parents want their children to have cell phone access at school (Hunter, 2007). School officials can set up a cell phone safety line for students to use when walking to and from school. Students call the safety line from their cell phone before they leave school and describe approximately how long it should take for them to get home. Once home, students call the safety line again to say they have made it home safely. If the student is not heard from in an appropriate amount of time, a worker at the safety line can call the student's cell phone. If the student does not answer, the safety line staff will call the appropriate authorities to locate the child. Parents, community volunteers, and even older high school students can run the safety line. The safety line may help ease the anxiety of working parents who worry about their children being secure on their way to and from school.

During fire drills, tornado alarms, and other schoolwide emergency drills, it is the teachers' job to keep track of their students. During this inevitable chaos, cell phones are a great way to quickly find a student who may be lost or unaccounted for, as opposed to the current method of running around trying to find the missing students with a bullhorn.

Tragedies such as the 1999 Columbine High School shootings and the 2007 Virginia Tech massacre remind us how important it is to have a way to instantly communicate with a large school community. Universities often use e-mail as their form of mass communication, but not all students check their e-mail on a regular basis. Most students do, however, have their cell phones with them at all times. This means that school or university officials could send out an instant text or voice message to all the student and faculty cell phones so that they are made aware of any security concerns on campus. A Web resource called Rave (www.ravewireless. com) allows school officials to send out simultaneous instant text, e-mail, and/or recorded voice-message alerts to student, faculty, and staff cell phones.

Secondary students often struggle with teenage issues, everything from self-image concerns to thoughts of suicide to peer pressure. Some teenagers are reluctant to talk to their parents or even their friends about their concerns. Many school counselors have set up anonymous teen hotlines, which students can use their cell phones to access. Administrators could go one step further and set up text-messaging help lines, allowing students to text questions to trained teens or counselors. Students may find this comforting because it allows for more anonymity (they do not actually have to speak with someone, but can still receive help and advice). Additionally, the text messaging would allow counselors to keep a record of the texts from a phone.

Mobile Citizen Journalism

A Web site called People's 311 (www.peoples311.com) asks citizens to post mobile pictures of dangerous situations in New York City that need to be cleaned up or repaired. Some of the images include illegal advertisements posted on street corners or ivy that has overgrown onto the street and causes problems for vehicles. Citizens take a picture with their camera phone and send it to a Flickr map, where the picture appears at the correct location in New York City along with a short description of the problem. This same project could be conducted in schools or for the surrounding community.

The school staff could create a community Flickr account and give students the mobile Flickr address (see chapter 4 for a tutorial). Then students could snap images with their cell phones of dangerous situations in their own school or the surrounding community. For example, students could visually document wires hanging in a classroom or slippery floors. This activity allows students to take responsibility and initiative in keeping their school and surrounding community safe and clean. It also promotes mobile citizen journalism, which has become popular with the rise of cell phones. Mobile citizen journalism is everyday people documenting significant events and situations. When schools support this activity, students learn how to document newsworthy events and situations and contribute to keeping their school secure.

Student Absenteeism

Another management issue for teachers is student absenteeism. It is not easy for teachers to keep track of which students have missed lessons and it can be even more difficult to catch them up, especially at the secondary level, where many teachers interact with more than 100 students in one school day. Cell phones provide a potential solution for students who are absent from class. Students who are home sick can use their cell phone to call in to class during an open conference call using FreeConferencePro. Students can even participate in class from their sick bed because FreeConferencePro allows for a two-way real-time conference. If the absent student is unable to listen during the live conference call, the student can simply listen to the MP3 from FreeConferencePro at a more convenient time. This makes catching up a lot easier for students, and makes managing the information students have missed a lot easier for teachers. In addition, parents may appreciate being able to listen to the podcasts along with their children to help them with homework and class-related questions.

Qipit (www.qipit.com) is a free Web 2.0 resource that turns a cell phone into a copy machine and PDF converter. Anyone can use a mobile phone to take a picture of handwritten notes, whiteboards, or printed documents and send them to Qipit, where the image is immediately converted to a legible PDF document. This is handy for students who have missed class, because the teacher (or another student) can take a picture of the lecture notes or whiteboard activity and then have it immediately converted to a PDF document, which can be shared online, printed, or sent to a mobile phone.

Teacher Absenteeism

Students often do not perform at an optimum level when the teacher is out of school for a conference or because of illness. While substitute teachers do their best to keep students on task, they are often unaware of the classroom learning goals and thus students do not progress as quickly. YouMail's private voice-mail and greeting service could be a useful tool for teachers who are out sick. Instead of students receiving a "busy work" assignment from a substitute and then the teacher having an abundance of work to grade upon return, students can receive their assignments directly from the teacher's unique cell phone greeting, such as an audio assignment that must be posted before the end of class by calling in to the teacher's voice mail.

The teacher could check the voice mail and grade the assignments while away, by providing text-message feedback from YouMail to the students. The teacher could even assign individual activities to students to work on the next day in class (if the teacher is out again). This may help keep students on task when they have a substitute.

Moreover, the teacher could conduct or have their students participate in virtual cell phone conferences when they have a substitute using FreeConferencePro. The teacher could ask an "expert" to be a virtual guest speaker, and students would participate in a conference with the virtual speaker during class on their cell phones. Since the conferences can be saved as MP3 files, the teacher, even while absent, can document who participated in the conference. The teacher could also create an assessment based on the phone conference to make sure that students fully participated and learned from their experience.

Struggling Students

Most of today's classrooms include students with varying abilities and needs. No one teacher is equipped to handle the needs of every individual student, and teachers often rely on a support system of parents and special education specialists. Now mobile devices can help as well. With Gabcast and cell phones, teachers can record class sessions, which can be a boon to struggling students and their support personnel. Students who need more time to comprehend the information presented in class can download and listen to the podcasts as many times as needed. Special education instructors and parents who are helping students can also listen to the podcasts to learn about class assignments and activities. Of course, we can currently record classes with videocameras or tape recorders, but the results cannot immediately be posted to the Web, where others can access them. These technologies require a lot more work than simply using the cell phone.

At the secondary level, the content becomes increasingly difficult for some students and parents. Using FreeConferencePro, parents can call in to class when the course is in session to ask any necessary questions, or they can put their phone on mute and listen to the class session to have a better sense of course content.

Connecting with Parents

According to the 2006 NetDay Speak Up report (Project Tomorrow, 2006b), many teachers are looking for technology solutions that will help them communicate better with parents. As mentioned before, teachers can document their class activities with Gabcast podcasts, which parents can download to help their children. Cell phones can aid in parent communication in other ways as well. Phone conferences, for instance, are very common today. With the addition of FreeConferencePro, teachers can document the phone conferences with parents (stored privately, of course) so that they have a record of everything said in the conversation. While most parents are very supportive, FreeConferencePro is also helpful when working with the more difficult parents who may later return and claim that the conversation did not occur.

Teachers can also take advantage of the simplicity of Jott mobile messaging. Simply create a contact list with all the parents' e-mail addresses and cell phone numbers, and then whenever you need to inform parents about a class assignment or issue, just send a Jott message. Teachers can do this anywhere on a cell phone (they don't have to be at their computer).

Homework Help

To provide homework help, secondary teachers could set up virtual office hours. Although some secondary teachers currently do this with instant-messaging forums, many students do not have access to the Internet outside of school and therefore cannot participate. When teachers take advantage of cell phones and FreeConferencePro, students needing homework help can call in at specified times (such as from 7:00 to 8:00 in the evening each night or every other night). Teachers do not need to have Internet access at home in order to help the students. Because FreeConferencePro has a recording feature, teachers can keep help sessions on file. The MP3 files could also be posted to the class Web site to create a podcast library of help topics. This could be used as a reference for students.

Teachers could ask students from previous years who understand the content well to be part of the virtual office hours. This alleviates some burden on teachers and gives older students opportunities to practice their content knowledge. A high-school classroom, for instance, could team up with an elementary- or middle-school classroom (for example in mathematics). The high-school students could take turns being on the homework helpline, and the younger students could call in with their questions.

Teachers could also set up a text-messaging helpline (similar to the libraries with text-messaging services mentioned in chapter 6). Students could text message the teacher or trained students during certain hours for quick homework help.

Chapter 8

Cell Phones in Preschool and Lower Elementary Learning

Although the focus of this book is on cell phones as learning tools for secondary students, cell phones also have potential as learning tools for preschool and elementary students. Although many argue (and it is a valid argument) that PK–5 students do not have their own cell phones, those statistics are rapidly changing. Amoroso (2006) estimates that by 2010, 54% of 8–12 year olds will have their own cell phone. Hunter (2007) describes parents' reasons for giving younger children cell phones: Safety and communication are significant concerns—parents want to be able to keep track of their children at all times. Parents also think cell phones allow them to have a better connection with their children. Cell phones allow parents to call their children at any time to talk about their day.

Although Hunter (2007) also found that some parents oppose giving their younger children cell phones, considering the growing number of elementary-age children with cell phones, I think it is reasonable to consider how cell phones could be learning tools for younger students. In addition, educational organizations are starting to research and develop educational software for cell phones targeted at young children. Basic literacy skills such as reading and arithmetic are the focus of these efforts. One example by PBS Kids is called the "Ready to Learn Cell Phone Study" (Horowitz et al., 2006). The researchers loaded parents' cell phones with software designed to help preschoolers learn their alphabet. Ultimately they found that cell phones were effective tools for delivering the PBS preschool Ready to Learn content to preschoolers. Therefore it is not ridiculous to begin to consider how cell phones could be used as learning tools for younger children.

Etiquette Starts Early

As mentioned in earlier chapters, one big complaint expressed by adults concerning cell phones and teenagers is that they are using them inappropriately. Teenagers are frequently text messaging or talking while they are driving; they text during movies, speeches, and church services; and they often overspend their minutes. By the time students reach the secondary level, they have already developed many poor cell phone habits. Early intervention may be the key to help students develop appropriate cell phone etiquette and budget management. Using a cell phone could be compared to driving a car. While the age to obtain a license in most states is 16, students with parent supervision and certified driving instructors can start learning to drive earlier (usually 15).

Instead of just giving teenagers cell phones for the first time and having them incur overcharges for too much text messaging because they don't understand their phone plans, or getting in trouble at school for taking inappropriate pictures because they were never taught cell phone etiquette, children could be exposed to appropriate uses long before they have their own phone. This could happen under the supervision of teachers and parents. In addition, the cell phone can first be introduced to younger students as a learning tool rather than a social toy.

Additionally, teachers could send home guidelines for parents to help them talk with their children about cell phone etiquette. Figure 8.1 presents a sample letter home concerning cell phone etiquette.

Figure 8.1 Sample cell phone etiquette letter

Dear Parents and Guardians:

The students are currently doing a homework assignment with an option to include a cell phone. At Anyschool, we are teaching students that cell phones are not just social toys, but learning tools for professional growth and development. We are modeling curriculum-based activities in which cell phones help with data collection and learning. We want to encourage you to participate in the optional cell phone activities with your children.

This is also an opportunity for all of us to teach cell phone etiquette to the children. Every year the average age that children start using a cell phone and receive their first cell phone gets younger and younger. As a result, it is important to talk with children before they get a cell phone about how to appropriately use one, and how to stay safe when using one, so that when they do get their first cell phone, they will already be well educated on how to use it. Children also need to be made aware of the cost of owning a cell phone. While I encourage you talk with your children, I realize that sometimes it is helpful to have some ideas on how to start this process (if you have not already done so). The following list describes cell phone topics that are important to go over with younger children, and tips on teaching children how to use cell phones appropriately.

1. Help your children understand the cost of a cell phone. Go over your cell phone plan with your children, so they understand the costs associated with using the tool. Explain, for example, that "every time Mom sends a text message, it costs Mom 10 cents." You could even have a "text-message bank," where you put in a dime every time you help your children send a text message so they can see the relationship between the text message and the cost. To help your children understand the costs of calling and overcharges on minutes, you can give them a certain number of minutes that they can use your cell phone each day or week (such as five or ten minutes). If they want to use it more, they have to give you a few cents or do a chore.

2. Talk about when it is appropriate and inappropriate to make and receive calls or text messages. Together with your kids, create a rules chart that

Continued

Figure 8.1, *Continued*

describes where and when kids (and parents!) are allowed to make and receive calls and text messages. For example, it could say:

- You may only call and text message people you know and who are approved by Mom or Dad.

- You may not make or receive calls or text messages during meal times.

- You may make and receive calls and text messages only between 8:00 am and 8:00 pm.

- You may only make emergency calls and text messages at other times.

- You may not make or receive calls or text messages when you are in a public place and it may disturb others around you. This includes the movie theater, library, and church.

- You should always get the approval of Mom or Dad before sending a picture or video of yourself, a friend, or a family member to someone else.

Make sure you also talk about the reasons why calls or text messages should not be made during certain times, such as the potential for waking someone up if you call too late in the evening.

3. Talk with your children about how they speak and text message on the cell phone.

- You do not need to speak loudly.

- Be aware that people around you can hear your conversation, so be careful about the information you are giving out (such as your home address or even your name).

- You should not call or text message someone when you are in the middle of a conversation with someone else.

Again, make sure you also talk about the reasons why they should or should not speak or text message a certain way on the cell phone. For instance, point out that it is polite to pay full attention to the person who is speaking to you.

Student Ownership

One important aspect to consider is that students themselves do not need to have their own cell phones in order to take advantage of them as learning tools. Keep in mind that most elementary-age children do not own their own computers, yet we do not ignore the fact that the computer can be a useful learning tool for younger students. There are many one-computer classrooms where innovative teachers employ one computer for 30 students; the same can be done for cell phones. If the classroom teacher has a cell phone, that would be enough. Many activities can be done with just one cell phone. It is also unnecessary for students to use cell phones inside the classroom. The following sections detail activities that can be conducted inside and outside the classroom with one cell phone.

One Cell Phone Outside the Classroom

Field Trips

As mentioned previously, cell phones can be useful during field trips for data collection, to record sounds, interviews, or observations. While each elementary student probably does not have a personal cell phone, the parent volunteers and teachers usually do. Students can be placed in groups of four or five with a parent volunteer or teacher with a cell phone to complete a project. For example, young elementary students going to a farm or zoo can record animal sounds using Gabcast, Jott, Gcast, or Hipcast. When the students are back at school, the teacher can download the audio and let the students try to identify the sounds they are hearing. The students could also take pictures of the animals with the cell phone and have them sent directly to the class Flickr site. Then the students could try to match the sounds with the animals. To extend the activity, the teacher could download the MP3 audio files and Flickr photos, and put them into a video editor (such as iMovie or Movie Maker) to create a movie of the trip with authentic sound effects and student reactions. This makes a nice present to send home to parents or to present to them at parents night.

Homework with Parents

Parents often like to find ways to be involved with what their children are studying. Homework assignments that use cell phones can be opportunities for parents to become more involved in their young children's education. For example, teachers often ask students to find different biological phenomena in nature and bring them to school. Cell phones could be very handy for this assignment with younger children. Teachers could have children locate different types of trees or insects and take pictures of them with their parents' cell phones. Teachers could give parents instructions on how to send the pictures, along with a quick text message of what the images are, to the class Flickr page.

One Cell Phone Inside the Classroom

Activity Centers

Teachers may find it useful to use one cell phone as a "center" or "station" in an elementary classroom. For example, students individually can easily go to the cell phone station to create a class podcast that broadcasts the highlights of learning activities that occurred throughout the week. With Gcast, students simply record their portion of the newscast into the cell phone. Then the teacher can log in to Gcast and create a playlist of all of the newscasts recorded. Parents can subscribe to Gcast to hear the weekly update. Another activity could be to take advantage of the camcorder feature on many cell phones, since some schools do not have camcorders or do not let younger students use them. At the cell phone center, students could make short films, such as public service announcements. They could send them (with their teacher's help) to Eyespot and export them to their parents' e-mail accounts.

Sending Projects Home

Elementary students are notorious for creating numerous art projects in class, some of which they can take home (such as sculptures) and some of which they cannot (such as class murals). The class projects that students cannot take home are not always shared with parents. Teachers can take advantage of Web 2.0 sites that send images by allowing students to send pictures of class projects to their parents' cell phones. For example, Pix2Fone (see chapter 4) could be used to send students' artwork to their parents' cell phone, then parents could use the artwork as their background wallpaper. In addition, preschool or kindergarten students could create holiday or birthday cards in class with Kid Pix or other user-friendly art tool, export them as a picture file, and send them to their parents' cell phones.

Chapter 9

The Future of Cell Phones in Schools

In 2004, the initial age of owning a cell phone was between 11 and 15 years, and 87% of the U.S. population owned cell phones (Selian & Srivastava, 2004). These statistics demonstrate that not only are cell phones ubiquitous in our culture, the age of adoption is only going to decrease with time, and it will not be uncommon to see elementary students with their own cell phones. Furthermore, young adults want their cell phones to be the "communications Swiss Army knife" (Rainie & Keeter, 2006), suggesting that cell phone features will only become more complex. Currently we have cell phones that can surf the Internet, check e-mail, text message, take photos, play basic games, capture short video, play ringtones, store small amounts of data, and record audio messages. As we have already seen with the introduction of the iPhone in 2007, all of these cell phone features will be greatly improved over the next few years. Before long, it will no longer be an option to have a camcorder or Web-browsing capabilities on a cell phone; it will simply be a standard feature. This chapter discusses the future of cell phones in learning and how cell phones will become more adaptable to classroom instruction.

Educational Software

In the future more software companies will be developing products for cell phones. In addition, software and education organizations are considering all ages of students appropriate for cell phone educational software. For example, as mentioned in chapter 8, PBS Kids recently teamed up with the Sesame Workshop, Sprint, WestEd, and GoTV Networks to create software for cell phones to help preschoolers learn their ABC's (Horowitz et al., 2006). Parents had the software on their cell phone and would let the kids use the cell phone to play with the software.

In addition, universities and educational companies are starting to develop content-specific software such as Math4Mobile (www.math4mobile.com), created by the Institute for Alternatives in Education in cooperation with Education Faculty at the University of Haifa. Math4Mobile is free software that can be loaded onto cell phones. The software is developed for students in Grades 5–12. Another example is MoneyManager (www.8mobile.org/moneyManager.aspx), which allows people to track their financial transactions on their cell phones. While not created specifically for the classroom, MoneyManager can easily be adapted for classroom use. Business and economic teachers may find MoneyManager a useful piece of software for their students' cell phones.

Using cell phone software may allow for better connections between the real world and the classroom. Chapter 5 mentions tools that can help teachers create class Web sites and homework reminders for cell phones. Eventually course management software will be on cell phones, and teachers will be able to simply send a grade report directly to the cell phones of students and parents.

Writing, Literature, and Textbooks

The idea of writing a story for a cell phone is not so far-fetched. Recently in Japan a young author typed her entire 142-page novel on her cell phone, and it has since become a bestseller (Norrie, 2007). The author not only wrote it on her cell phone, but she published it in a mobile format and has sold more than 420,000 mobile copies (subscribers download the text and read it on their cell phones). The 21-year-old author claimed she started writing books on her cell phone when she was in middle school. According to Norrie (2007), mobile novels have become extremely popular in Japan.

Web sites such as Wattpad (http://wattpad.com) allow anyone to upload and share their original stories and novels and create a digital version that can easily be downloaded to most cell phones. BooksInMyPhone (http://booksinmyphone. com) has a large collection of classic literature that can be downloaded to any cell phone for reading. Although many people may struggle with reading on the tiny screens, it seems that mobile novels will become more popular in the coming years. It is even possible that schools that have started to use more digital textbooks could eventually make mobile versions so students can have access to their textbooks at any time.

MP3 Players, Recorders, and Radios

Recently Apple introduced the iPhone (www.apple.com/iphone/), which is an all-in-one computer cell phone system. Beyond the basic cell phone features, the iPhone includes an MP3 player. There is no need to buy a separate MP3 player with this new iPhone, and probably the cell phones of the future. Students could create and listen to podcasts right on their cell phone. Recently Sprint teamed up with MobiTV (www.mobitv.com) to allow real-time TV programs to be downloaded to a cell phone and viewed anytime. There may no longer be a need to take hours of class time to watch a feature-length film if students can do it for homework on their cell phones. This means that eventually the cell phone can be used as a VCR or DVR, and students can set their cell phones to record a PBS show at a certain time and watch it for homework.

Cell phone companies such as Nokia are already creating cell phones with radio antennas built into them. People will no longer need to purchase a special FM or XM radio for their car or home; they can simply use their cell phone to listen to their favorite radio station. If students were given an NPR assignment, they would set their cell phone alarm, and then listen to the broadcast wherever they were when the alarm went off, because students seldom are away from their favorite toy.

Live Streaming, Audio Editing, and Video Editing

AT&T has developed cell phones with "video share" (http://tinyurl.com/3bsjgy), which allows people to record a video with their cell phone camcorder and then stream it live to another cell phone. This is just the beginning of live mobile television. At MobiTV (http://mobitv.com) for a price of $9.99 per month, you can receive television programming from around the world on your mobile phone. This could have a huge effect on foreign language and social studies classes studying various cultures. Students will have immediate access to foreign programming, which will give them insight into other cultures.

Moreover, there is a good chance that cell phones will eventually have features that allow you to edit your captured photographs, audio recordings, and video files right on the cell phone. Students will no longer need iMovie or Movie Maker to create a class movie; rather, they will capture, edit, and export their films or storybooks right from their phone. Teachers need not worry about reserving computer lab time or taking away from important instructional time. In addition, students will no longer need to worry about having access to the same computer to work on their huge video file each day, because they will complete their entire video assignment from their cell phone for homework. When students complete their homework, they can send the video file to their teacher's cell phone or the class Web site. Teachers will grade student projects right on their cell phone from anywhere, rather than having to be on a specific computer or reviewing a stack of CDs or DVDs.

Surveillance systems have also been created for cell phones. SingTel (http://home.singtel.com/consumer/products/mobile/value_added_services/mobile_livecam_overview.asp), for instance, has developed a surveillance service that allows users to monitor their homes remotely using their cell phones. While it is controversial, these live video devices could be used for classroom surveillance. They could also be used to support classroom instruction. Parents who want to help their children with their homework assignments and students who are absent could watch the class activities on their mobile devices.

Live video on cell phones could become very useful at high school athletic events. Purdue University is one of the first athletic programs to allow the fans attending the football game to "call up" instant replays on their cell phones ("On Demand," 2007). This could have a large effect on athletics and the people attending the games.

This technology has the potential to trickle down to the high school level, allowing parents and students to "call up" instant replays on their cell phones.

GPS Tools and Tracking

In today's society we put computer chips in our pets to locate them if they are lost. It only makes sense to use GPS (Global Positioning System) chips in cell phones. GPS chips have been in cell phones since 2002 so that phone owners could be located in case of emergency, but only recently has the technology become available to use cell phones as tracking devices (Nickson, 2005). Of course, the locator chips are helpful if you lose a cell phone or need to find a child, but the GPS tracking capabilities in the newer phones can also be utilized for classroom projects. For example, students studying geography can use their GPS cell phones as mapping tools to help them get from one location to another. When cell phones are used for tracking, students can learn some very important life skills.

At Wayfinder (www.wayfinder.com) you will discover that GPS software for cell phones includes such features as voice navigation (similar to the built-in car navigation systems), speed limit warnings for driving, and up-to-date global mobile maps with a world atlas and destination points of interest. In the near future, students in a foreign language or social studies class studying culture will be able to simply use their cell phones to create a travel log or travel brochure that includes places to visit, maps, and even local entertainment. Students learning to drive can use their cell phones to keep them safe by taking advantage of the built-in driving tools (such as the traffic warnings, speed limit changes, and instant driving directions). Wouldn't we prefer that students learn to use cell phones safely in cars rather than employ them only as toys for chatting and other distractions?

Digital Projectors

Some cell phones are currently being built as high-definition digital projection tools (Bullis, 2006). This means that cell phones will eventually be able to project television and computer screens in high definition. This could have a huge effect on schools. Schools will no longer need to purchase expensive LCD projectors for every classroom to display computer monitors or television screens; teachers will simply plug in their own cell phone to the computer, DVR, or TV to view the content. Teachers will no longer have to check out projectors or worry about bulbs burning out (which can be an expensive fix). The cell phone has the potential to become the inexpensive LCD projector of the future.

Faxes and Scanners

Although most cell phones are still fairly basic, some can be used as a fax, copier, or scanner. The Web 2.0 resources Qipit (www.qipit.com) and scanR (www.scanr.com) allow anyone with a certain type of cell phone (depending on the resolution of the camera in the phone) to fax, copy, and scan. You can take a picture with your cell phone and send it directly to the scanR account, where the image is turned into a PDF document. You can then send it to any e-mail account. Once it is a PDF document, it can be downloaded and edited with a PDF editor. In addition, you can send the scanned document to any fax machine in the world.

Although this service really works well only with specific cell phones, as cell phones improve, we may not need to have faxes and scanners anymore. Students may soon learn how to use their cell phone in new ways to communicate in the business world, scanning work-related documents and sending faxes. Cell phones could also be used as professional tools for future job searches. Students may be able to scan their résumés and fax them without using a computer.

Mobile Storage

Many schools have a hard time storing student data (especially larger video and image files). In the future, this may no longer be an issue, as storage on cell phones is expected to increase. Just as iPods can be used as devices to save and transfer files, cell phones will soon have gigabytes of storage space. The iPhone, introduced in 2007, has the capacity to hold up to 16 GB, and this is sure to grow with time. There may be no more need to use thumb drives, Zip disks, or blank CDs to store school data. Students can simply take out their cell phone and store their valuable data right on their all-in-one communications device. For the last couple of years Samsung has been putting out cell phones with hard drive storage space and AT&T (http://mobilebackup.att.com/)has a mobile backup system for important phone numbers.

E-Commerce

According to Nickson (2005), cell phones will soon allow people to participate in many of the activities they enjoy doing online. Online shopping and e-commerce will soon be conducted easily with a cell phone. People will be able to purchase items using the cell phone as the wallet (charge it to my cell!). Students in an economics class studying the stock market could actually "trade" their stocks with their cell phones and get up-to-the-minute reports about their chosen stocks. Students in business, mathematics, or life-skills classes could learn how to do their online banking with their cell phones. Students may learn how to participate in online auction sites such as eBay and use them appropriately so they do not get "ripped off" or lose ratings as an eBay seller. A few Web sites, such as UnWired Buyer (www.unwiredbuyer.com), already let people conduct eBay and auction transactions on a cell phone.

Nokia has developed a phone that allows anyone to snap a picture of an item they want to purchase and then the item will automatically be ordered online (Morton, 2007). In other words, a phone that shops! While you are shopping with your cell phone, you will also be able to try on items virtually, a mobile fitting. For example, in Japan's Megane Top (or Top Glasses) superstore, customers can take a picture of their face with their cell phone, then combine it with images of different styles of glasses (Fallon, 2007). A Web site called IQzone (www.iqzone.com) allows anyone to create their own classified advertisements using a mobile phone. They can also manage their account through their cell phone.

Additionally, many new cell phones feature the ability to use RFID (radio-frequency identification) tags, which means that people can easily use their cell phones to pay for purchases (like a mobile credit card). At Slippery Rock University, students receive an RFID tag to attach to their cell phones. This tag allows them to pay for everything on campus and in the surrounding town such as movies and laundry services (Swedberg, 2007). With RFID technology, students could go online to keep track of all purchases. Students in economics or business classes could use this mobile shopping technology to do price comparisons. They could use their mobile camera to take pictures of items and find out the cost at different stores.

Point and Click

Nokia has been developing Point&Find technology, which allows users to take a picture of something with their cell phone camera and receive instant information about that item on their cell phone (Dugdale, 2007). For example, anyone could click a picture of a restaurant marquee and get immediate reviews about that particular restaurant on their cell phone. This will also be very useful when people are traveling to other countries and need to understand signage or restaurant menus in a foreign language. People could take a picture of a restaurant menu and receive an immediate translation of the menu items. This could be a useful device for foreign language teachers. In social studies, students could use their cell phones to "point and click" a local historical monument and get immediate information on that monument. Science teachers who are studying the ecosystem can have students take images of different natural objects and receive immediate information about the object.

Assistive Technology

Pilotfish and Synaptics have released a prototype of a cell phone that has no buttons (Kharif, 2006). The phone relies on signs and gestures by using a sensitive touchpad. These touchpads will also make it easier to navigate the Internet using a cell phone and make cell phones in general more user friendly. While the touchpad phone is still a prototype, think of the potential for students with hearing impairments or dexterity issues using the tiny cell phone buttons. While students with hearing difficulties can text message to get their ideas across, they cannot independently fully participate in audio conversations. That may change with the new generation of cell phones. These cell phones may also include closed captioning so that students with hearing difficulties can have a "verbal" conversation with a non-hearing-impaired person on the other end. Real-time video can be integrated so the students see the lip movement of the speaker on the other phone. This may mean that cell phones become the new iSight or virtual videoconferencing tool.

For students with visual impairments, a few pricey products on the market, such as Nuance Talks (www.nuance.com/talks/), will convert any cell phone text into an audio file. Nuance Zooms software (www.nuance.com/zooms/) allows screen magnification on many cell phones. Software such as this will greatly aid students who have difficulty using tiny cell phone screens. With this technology, students with visual impairments can better participate in e-mail, text messaging, and Web surfing, and will have more ease in using cell phone tools such as calendars and calculators.

The benefit of cell phone assistive technologies over computer assistive technologies is that the cell phone is a tool the students will have with them for their entire life, inside and outside of school. Students will not have to lug around a laptop or even a larger PDA device; they will have an all-in-one independent aid with them at all times. In addition, students will not have to rely on the computer as their verbal aid system; they can simply become comfortable with one tool that does it all.

Starter Phones and Phone Plans

Cell phones are being developed for students of all ages. Companies such as LeapFrog (http://mytictalk.com/LeapFrog/) are introducing "starter phones" for young children that have limited buttons. Features include children being allowed to call only those numbers specifically programmed into their phone by their parents, children being allowed to call only during assigned permissible times of the day, and parents having the ability to disable the phone at any time. These starter devices provide younger children with the opportunity to learn how to use cell phones, and allow parents to control how much and when the cell phones are used.

AT&T recently introduced Smart Limits, a phone plan for parents to use with younger children (www.wireless.att.com/learn/articles-resources/parental-controls/smart-limits.jsp). The phone plan allows parents to set up a restricted number of calling minutes, times the phone can be used, and restricted access. AT&T will even send an alert to the child when the minute allotment for the month is running out and then shut off the phone (except for preapproved numbers) when the child reaches the designated minutes.

M-Government

Some developing nations are using cell phones to bring government to remote people (Lasica, 2007). While this is currently not a widespread cell phone technology, it is not crazy to predict that soon we may be able to participate in our democracy over cell phones. Such things as voting, renewing a driver's license, conducting a census, filing taxes, sending policy recommendations to political leaders, providing e-mail alerts about crimes in the local area, and other city, state, and federal duties may be conducted through mobile connections. According to the Mobile Generation Report (Lasica, 2007), mobile technology has the potential to completely change the relationship between citizens and public officials. Students in social studies classes may learn how to participate in a mobile democracy in the near future. Additionally, students may have opportunities to interact with political representatives through their mobile devices.

Solar-Powered Cell Phones

Science educators who are trying to get their students to "go green" may rejoice with the invention of solar-powered cell phones. The Japanese company NTT DoCoMo has developed a solar-powered flip cell phone ("Solar Powered Cell Phone," 2006). Solar-powered cell phones will not only save on energy, but also relieve students and teachers of the need to cart around electric plugs to continuously charge their phones. Hence, no more excuses that "my cell phone battery died!"

Chapter 10

More Web 2.0 Resources for Cell Phones

Although this book describes many Web 2.0 resources that work in conjunction with cell phones, many more Web 2.0 resources could be used for learning solutions. In this chapter, I briefly describe some of those resources. This is by no means an exhaustive list of Web 2.0 resources for cell phones, but it does give a sense of what is available (mostly for free) to any cell phone user.

Podcasting

Evoca

http://Evoca.com

Evoca allows anyone to record audio on their cell phone and permits up to 15 minutes of free recording at one time. Like the other podcasting sites, you can keep your recording private or make it public by publishing it to any blog or Web site. Unlike the other sites, you can pay $2.50 and order a transcript of your audio recording (this feature may be helpful for assistive learning). Additionally, you can search the recordings word for word (this may be a handy feature for teachers who are evaluating the audio and looking for specific topics).

BlogTalkRadio

http://cinch.blogtalkradio.com

BlogTalkRadio (or CINCH) allows anyone in the world to dial the BlogTalkRadio phone number and immediately record a podcast. Once the recording is finished, BlogTalkRadio automatically gives the podcast an RSS feed. Unlike other mobile podcasting tools, there is no need to create an account in BlogTalkRadio, so you can podcast from anywhere, even if you forgot to set up an account. While the BlogTalkRadio phone number is not toll free, this resource offers probably one of the easiest ways to make a podcast.

Utterz

http://utterz.com

Utterz is a free service that allows you to post images, videos, audio, or text from your cell phone to a private Utterz site or to a public blog or Web space. Utterz is essentially an "all-in-one" mobile media-posting service. While with other podcasting and photo-posting services you can post from many cell phones to one place on the Internet, Utterz allows you to post only from your own cell phone to the Internet. For individual mobile blogging or mobile journalism, Utterz is a powerful resource.

Voice Mail

Jangl

www.jangl.com

Jangl allows you to input the e-mail addresses of friends, then you receive a private phone number to call them. When you call on your cell phone using the private phone number, you can leave a voice mail that will immediately be sent to the friend's e-mail. Your friend will be given a number in the e-mail to call you back. This allows you to keep your real number private! Jangl might be nice for teachers who want students and parents to be able to contact them, but may not want them to have access to their private phone number. Also, it is good to teach students not to give away their real phone number. People who set up accounts in Jangl get a voice-mail box that will allow them to manage their calls online.

Conferencing

TalkShoe

www.talkshoe.com

TalkShoe is a free Internet resource that permits you to create an account for conference podcasting. You can have up to 250 people participate in a conference at one time. Additionally, the conference can be broadcast as a podcast live on TalkShoe's Web site so anyone can listen and participate (you can also set up private group accounts). TalkShoe also allows you to promote your podcast show. For instance, if students want to produce an authentic newscast that focuses on interviews or hot topics with expert guest speakers and goes out to the public, they could do this for free through TalkShoe.

Mobile Notes

Pinger

http://pinger.com

Pinger works with cell phones to record messages and notes. While Jott (mentioned in chapter 3) creates speech-to-text messages, Pinger creates voice messages. In other words, you cannot "read" the voice message left, but you can listen to it on your cell phone similar to voice mail, but with more benefits. For example, in Pinger you can send one voice message to a group of people. These group messages can be used for class alerts and instant pop quizzes for extra credit (first one to "ping" back the answer earns the points). Every ping that you create or that someone sends to you is automatically saved to a private account online, and it can be downloaded as a QuickTime file. Pinger does not give out phone numbers. This means that students will not have access to a teacher's cell phone number, but they can still leave the teacher a "Pinger" note. Furthermore, students can ping notes to each other without having to share personal phone numbers. Pinger sets up a local area code number for you, but it works around the world, so you can dial locally and call globally.

BrainCast

http://braincast.viatalk.com

BrainCast works in a similar fashion to Jott (see chapter 3). People can create a free account at BrainCast and then record audio messages using their cell phone. BrainCast stores all the audio messages as MP3 files in a private space on the site. Unlike Jott, BrainCast uses a toll-free number, which would allow students without cell phone access to use a landline if they were using BrainCast for homework (such as a brainstorming exercise). BrainCast also has a "reminder" feature, in which BrainCast calls you (or anyone else) and plays a verbal message that you recorded. This is a nice feature for students who are using their cell phones as an organizational tool. Students can set up BrainCast so that they receive reminder calls about deadlines and assignments. BrainCast does include an RSS feed if you want to make your notes public.

Mobile Web Sites

Winksite

www.winksite.com

Chapters 5 and 6 describe resources that allow you to build a mobile-friendly Web site. Winksite is another Web 2.0 resource that allows anyone to build a mobile-friendly Web site using a computer or their cell phone.

RSS, E-mail, and Favorites

Google and Yahoo Mobile

Google Mobile: www.google.com/intl/en_us/mobile/sms/
Yahoo Mobile: http://mobile.yahoo.com

Most of Google's services (such as e-mail, searching, calendar, mapping) and Yahoo's (such as Flickr, e-mail, searching, news, mapping) are available on some cell phones. While some of the services (such as Google Earth) really only seem to work on more expensive cell phones, such as iPhones or BlackBerry devices, in the near future they will probably be more widely available.

Flurry

www.flurry.com

Flurry is a free software application for the cell phone that provides mobile access to favorite Web sites, blogs, e-mail, and news resources. Flurry is similar to Plusmo (described in chapter 5). Users can create a free Flurry account, and then put in their favorite RSS feeds (to news sites or blogs or any site that has an RSS feed). Then on their cell phone they can easily access the sites by typing in their Flurry Web address.

Camera and Camcorder Resources

Last Spotted

www.lastspotted.com

Last Spotted is a free service, which asks you to "spy" or "search" for someone or something. Every time you see that person or thing, you can send a text message and/or picture to a Last Spotted account. You can use this site to set up "I-spy" curriculum-based games with your students. For example, you could create one called "Insects". Your students, who are studying insects in a biology class, can use their cell phone to take pictures of insects that they encounter in their everyday activities and send their pictures (along with a text message of what type of insect they think it is to the Last Spotted account). Students do not need to create an account in order to use Last Spotted. The teacher can set up the account (monitor it) and give the students the email address to send their pictures. My only major concern is that there does not seem to be a good way to keep the account private.

Radar

http://Radar.net

Radar is a free mobile photo- and video-sharing site. It allows anyone to send pictures and videos from a cell phone directly into a private Radar Web space. Radar also allows you to add "friends" to your account so that you can share pictures and videos by cell phone with each other and comment on the shared media.

Reference and Organizational Tools

MobileQuery

http://mobilequery.com

At MobileQuery you will find freelance reference applications for cell phones such as a spelling checker, dictionaries, a crossword puzzle finder, a thesaurus, stock quotes, and highway traffic information. The applications are easy to use on just about any basic cell phone.

Nozbe

http://nozbe.com

Nozbe allows anyone to create easy to-do lists using a computer or a cell phone. Nozbe couples with Jott (see chapter 3) so that anyone can call in to Jott and post a to-do task in their Nozbe account. Nozbe also has a mobile Web site (.mobi) for easy access by cell phone to your to-do list.

I Want Sandy

http://iwantsandy.com

Sandy is a virtual "personal assistant." First you create a free account at the I Want Sandy Web site, and then you can use Jott to call in your to-do list. Sandy text messages your cell phone to remind you of upcoming events and assignments.

Remember The Milk

http://Rememberthemilk.com

Using Remember The Milk and Jott, you can leave voice-to-text reminders in your Remember The Milk account. When it is time to be reminded, you will get a text message on your phone. This site also works with Apple iCal or Google Calendar to allow you to view your to-do list on your Web-ready cell phone. Furthermore, you can set up your reminders to go to friends and family. Teachers and parents could set up reminders to go to students.

Logos, Wallpaper, and Ringtones

PixDrop, Cellfish, and 3Guppies

www.pixdrop.com
www.cellfish.com
www.mobilatory.com

Chapter 5 discusses developing class projects for cell phones. One project involves students creating wallpaper and logo images to upload to their cell phones. PixDrop and Cellfish easily allow you send original pictures to a cell phone to use as a logo or wallpaper. Similar to Pix2Fone, you do not need to have an account in order to use PixDrop. Cellfish and Mobilatory also allow you to send ringtones and videos to your cell phone.

Text Messaging

Txt2day and txtDrop

www.txt2day.com

http://txtdrop.com

Chapter 5 explores ways to use online text-messaging services in learning. Txt2day and txtDrop allow anyone to send a text message from the Internet for free to just about any cell phone.

Mobile Shopping

Frucall

http://frucall.com

Students who are learning about comparison shopping and real-world applications may enjoy using Frucall, which allows you to find a product at the best possible price when out shopping. Frucall provides many opportunities for authentic activities in business and economics courses. Students can compare prices and learn about money management using this free downloadable software for cell phones.

Mobile Quizzes

MyBuddyQuiz

www.mybuddyquiz.com

Students may enjoy taking quizzes on their cell phones and even creating them using a free tool called MyBuddyQuiz. Students can create the quizzes online and then send to their cell phones, eliminating the need to bring cell phones into school. Please note MyBuddyQuiz seems to work best from a Microsoft Windows computer.

Music and Art

Ripple9

www.ripple9.com

Music teachers may benefit from Ripple9, which allows users to publish their original recordings and share upcoming concert information by cell phone. Students who have put together their own bands or music groups can create mobile advertisements concerning their upcoming gigs with Ripple9.

Chord Maestro

www.chordmaestro.com

Chord Maestro is free software that you can load onto many cell phones. Chord Maestro lets musicians who work with fretted instruments (such as a guitar) to use their mobile phone to learn new chords, write songs, or look up chords.

Myartspace

www.myartspace.org.uk

Myartspace allows students on field trips to collect images of their experience with their cell phones and post them to an online art gallery. Students can create their own galleries of their field trip experiences or they can search the many galleries on the site. The site offers an abundance of lesson plans for teachers that include how to set up their mobile art galleries with their students and how to best use this resource as a learning tool.

Health Education

myFoodPhone

www.myfoodphone.com

myFoodPhone allows people to keep track of their diets by getting their meals evaluated by a nutritionist. Participants take a picture with their cell phone of each meal they eat during the day. Then they send their images to myFoodPhone, which will provide feedback on how healthy their meals were. This would be a good project for any health class focusing on diet and nutrition and tracking calories.

References

Alvermann, D. E., & Xu, S. H. (2003). Children's everyday literacies: Intersections of popular culture and language arts instruction. *Language Arts, 81*(2), 145–54.

Amoroso, M. (2006). *Tween market has the potential to double by 2010.* Yankee Group. Retrieved from www.yankeegroup.com/ResearchDocument. do?id=14058

Bean, T. W., Bean, S. K., & Bean, K. F. (1999). Intergenerational conversations and two adolescents' multiple literacies: Implications for redefining content area literacy. *Journal of Adolescent & Adult Literacy, 42*(6), 438–448.

Becker, H. J. (2000, Fall/Winter). Who's wired and who's not: Children's access to and use of computer technology. *Children and Computer Technology, 10*(2), 44–75. Retrieved from www.futureofchildren.org/usr_doc/vol10no2art3.pdf

Bransford, J. D., Brown, A. L., & Cooking, R. R. (1999). *How people learn: Brain, mind, experience, and school.* Washington, DC: National Academy Press.

Britton, B. K., & Graesser, A. C. (Eds.). (1996). *Models of understanding text.* Mahwah, NJ: Lawrence Erlbaum Associates.

Bruce, B. C. (1997). Literacy technologies: What stance should we take? *Journal of Literacy Research, 29,* 289–309.

Bullis, K. (2006). High-definition TV from your cell phone. *Technology Review.* Retrieved from www.technologyreview.com/read_article.aspx?id=17395&ch=info tech

Cazden, C., & Leggett, E. (1981). Culturally responsive education: Recommendations for achieving Lau remedies II. In H. Trueba, G. Guthrie, and K. Au (Eds.), *Culture and the bilingual classroom: Studies in classroom ethnography* (pp. 69–86). Rowley, MA: Newbury House.

Cell phones and PDA's hit K–6. (2005, April). *Education Digest,* p. 52. (From Communicator, March 2005) Retrieved from http://tinyurl.com/3xqchy

Chandler-Olcott, K., & Mahar, D. (2003). "Tech-savviness" meets multiliteracies: Exploring adolescent girls' technology-mediated literacy practices. *Reading Research Quarterly, 38*(3), 356–385.

Children's Internet Protection Act. (2001). Federal Communications Commission. Retrieved from www.fcc.gov/cgb/consumerfacts/cipa.html

Cuban, L. (1986). *Teachers and machines: The classroom use of technology since 1920*. New York: Teachers College Press.

Cuban, L., Kirkpatrick, H., and Peck, C. (2001). High access and low use of technologies in high school classrooms: Explaining an apparent paradox. *American Educational Research Journal, 38*(4), 813–834.

Disney Mobile Survey. (2007, July). *Disney mobile survey: Teen and tween cell phone calls rise during the summer*. Retrieved from http://goliath.ecnext.com/coms2/summary_0199–6765233_ITM

Dugdale, A. (2007). *Future technology: Nokia's Point&Find technology both useful and creepy*. Retrieved from http://gizmodo.com/gadgets/future-technology/nokias-pointfind-technology-both-useful-and-creepy-314379.php

Fallon, S. (2007). *Cell phones: "Mobile fitting" lets you try on glasses via your cell phone*. Retrieved from http://gizmodo.com/gadgets/cell-phones/mobile-fitting-lets-you-try-on-glasses-via-your-cell-phone-312652.php

Finders, M. J. (1996). Queens and teen zines: Early adolescent females reading their way toward adulthood. *Anthropology & Education Quarterly, 27*(1), 71–89.

Gilroy, M. (2004). Invasion of the classroom cell phones. *Education Digest, 69*(6), 56–60.

Horowitz, J. E., Sosenko, L. D., Hoffman, J. L., Ziobrowski, J., Tafoya, A., Haagenson, A., & Hahn, S. (2006). *The PBS KIDS ready to learn cell phone study: Learning letters with Elmo*. Retrieved from www.pbs.org/readytolearn/research/cellphones.html

Hunter, A. (2007). *Should a 10-year-old have a cell phone?* Retrieved from http://tech.msn.com/guides/backtoschool/article.aspx?cp-documentid=5090290&GT1=10240

Jordan, C. (1985). Translating culture: From ethnographic information to educational program. *Anthropology and Education Quarterly, 16*, 105–123.

Kaiser Family Foundation. (2005). Generation M: Media in the lives of 8–18 year-olds. Retrieved from www.kff.org/entmedia/7251.cfm

Kharif, O. (2006). A quantum leap for cell phones. *Business Week*. Retrieved from www.businessweek.com/technology/content/aug2006/tc20060821_810437.htm

Kleiman, G. M. (2000, April–June). Myths and realities about technology in K–12 schools. *Leadership and the New Technologies, 14*. Retrieved April 7, 2004, from www2.edc.org/LNT/news/Issue14/featurecontents.htm

Lasica, J. D. (2007). *The mobile generation: Global transformations at the cellular level.* Retrieved from www.aspeninstitute.org/site/apps/ka/ec/product.asp?c= huLWJeMRKpH&b=667387&ProductID=416787

Lenhart, A., Madden, M., & Hitlin, P. (2005). *Teens and technology: Youth are leading the transition to a fully wired and mobile nation.* PEW Internet & American Life Project. Retrieved from www.pewinternet.org/PPF/r/162/report_display.asp

Lenhart, A., Madden, M., Rankin, A., & Smith, A. (2007). *Teens and social media: The use of social media gains a greater foothold in teen life as they embrace the conversational nature of interactive online media.* PEW Internet & American Life Project. Retrieved from www.pewinternet.org/PPF/r/230/report_display.asp

Levin, D., Arafeh, S., Lenhart, A., & Rainie, L. (2002). *The digital disconnect: The widening gap between Internet-savvy students and their schools.* PEW Internet & American Life Project. Retrieved from www.pewInternet.org/PPF/r/67/report_display.asp

Mohatt, G., & Erickson, F. (1981). Cultural differences in teaching styles in an Odawa school: A sociolinguistic approach. In H. Trueba, G. Guthrie, & K. Au (Eds.), *Culture and the bilingual classroom: Studies in classroom ethnography* (pp. 105–119). Rowley, MA: Newbury House.

Moje, E. B. (2000). "To be part of the story": The literacy practices of gangsta adolescents. *Teachers College Record, 102*(3), 652–690.

Moje, E. B. (2002). Re-framing adolescent literacy research for new times: Studying youth as a resource. *Reading Research and Instruction, 41*(3), 211–228.

Moje, E. B., & Sutherland, L. M. (2003). The future of middle school literacy education. *English Education, 35*(2), 149–164.

Morton, E. (2007). The sell phone for shoppers. *The Sun.* Retrieved from www.thesun.co.uk/sol/homepage/news/article576679.ece

National Center for Missing and Exploited Children. (2006). *Wireless Amber Alerts.* Retrieved from www.wirelessamberalerts.org/index.jsp

National School Safety and Security Services. (2007). *Cell phones can detract from school safety & crisis preparedness.* Retrieved from www.schoolsecurity.org/trends/cell_phones.html

Nickson, C. (2005). *The future of cell phones.* Retrieved from http://news.digitaltrends.com/featured_article34_page3.html

Norrie, J. (2007). In Japan, cellular storytelling is all the rage. *The Sydney Morning Herald.* Retrieved from www.smh.com.au/news/mobiles—handhelds/in-japan-cellular-storytelling-is-all-the-rage/2007/12/03/1196530522543.html

On demand FB cell phone replays created. (2007, September 27). *United Press International.* Retrieved from www.upi.com/NewsTrack/Science/2007/09/27/on_demand_fb_cell_phone_replays_created/9790/

O'Reilly, T. (2005). *What is Web 2.0: Design patterns and business models for the next generation of software.* Retrieved from www.oreillynet.com/pub/a/oreilly/tim/news/2005/09/30/what-is-Web-20.html

Papert, S. (1980). *Mindstorms: Children, computers and powerful ideas.* New York: Basic Books.

Prensky, M. (2001). Digital natives, digital immigrants. *On the Horizon. NCB University Press, 9*(5). Retrieved from www.marcprensky.com/writing

Project Tomorrow. (2006a). NetDay Speak Up 2006: K–12 student national findings. Retrieved from www.tomorrow.org/speakup/speakup_reports.html

Project Tomorrow. (2006b). NetDay Speak Up 2006: Teacher national findings. Retrieved from www.tomorrow.org/speakup/speakup_reports.html

Rainie, L. (2006). *Life online: Teens and technology and the world to come.* Speech to annual conference of Public Library Association, Boston. Retrieved from www.pewInternet.org/PPF/r/63/presentation_display.asp

Rainie, L., & Keeter, S. (2006). How Americans use their cell phones. PEW Internet & American Life Project. Retrieved from www.pewInternet.org/PPF/r/179/report_display.asp

Rosen, L. (2006). *Adolescents in MySpace: Identity formation, friendship and sexual predators.* Retrieved from www.csudh.edu/psych/lrosen.htm

Sedlak, A. J., Finkelhor, D., Hammer, H., & Schultz, D. J. (2002). *National estimates of missing children: An overview.* National Incidence Studies of Missing, Abducted, Runaway, and Thrownaway Children. Retrieved from www.ncjrs.gov/html/ojjdp/nismart/01/ns4.html

Selian, A., & Srivastava, L. (2004). *Mobile phones & youth: A look at the U.S. student market.* Retrieved from www.itu.int/osg/spu/ni/futuremobile/presentations/srivastava_youth_original.pdf

Solar powered cell phone charges free in sun. (2006, December 21). *The Raw Feed.* Retrieved from www.therawfeed.com/2006/12/solar-powered-cell-phone-charges-free.html

Soloway, E., Guzdial, M., & Hay, K. (1994). Learner-centered design: The challenge for HCI in the 21st century. *Interactions, 1*(2), 36–48.

Swedberg, C. (2007, July 6). Slippery rock adds RFID to student cell phones. *RFID Journal.* Retrieved from www.rfidjournal.com/article/articleview/3463/1/1/

Tell, C. (2000). Generation What? Connecting with today's youth. *Educational Leadership, 57*(4), 8–13.

Wikipedia. (2006). *Podcast.* Retrieved from http://en.wikipedia.org/wiki/Podcast/

Wikipedia. (2008). *Geotagging.* Retrieved from http://en.wikipedia.org/wiki/GeoTagging

National Educational Technology Standards for Students (NETS•S)

The National Educational Technology Standards for students are divided into six broad categories. Standards within each category are to be introduced, reinforced, and mastered by students. Teachers can use these standards as guidelines for planning technology-based activities in which students achieve success in learning, communication, and life skills.

1. Creativity and Innovation

Students demonstrate creative thinking, construct knowledge, and develop innovative products and processes using technology. Students:

  a. apply existing knowledge to generate new ideas, products, or processes

  b. create original works as a means of personal or group expression

  c. use models and simulations to explore complex systems and issues

  d. identify trends and forecast possibilities

2. Communication and Collaboration

Students use digital media and environments to communicate and work collaboratively, including at a distance, to support individual learning and contribute to the learning of others. Students:

  a. interact, collaborate, and publish with peers, experts, or others employing a variety of digital environments and media

  b. communicate information and ideas effectively to multiple audiences using a variety of media and formats

  c. develop cultural understanding and global awareness by engaging with learners of other cultures

  d. contribute to project teams to produce original works or solve problems

3. Research and Information Fluency

Students apply digital tools to gather, evaluate, and use information. Students:

a. plan strategies to guide inquiry

b. locate, organize, analyze, evaluate, synthesize, and ethically use information from a variety of sources and media

c. evaluate and select information sources and digital tools based on the appropriateness to specific tasks

d. process data and report results

4. Critical Thinking, Problem Solving, and Decision Making

Students use critical-thinking skills to plan and conduct research, manage projects, solve problems, and make informed decisions using appropriate digital tools and resources. Students:

a. identify and define authentic problems and significant questions for investigation

b. plan and manage activities to develop a solution or complete a project

c. collect and analyze data to identify solutions and make informed decisions

d. use multiple processes and diverse perspectives to explore alternative solutions

5. Digital Citizenship

Students understand human, cultural, and societal issues related to technology and practice legal and ethical behavior. Students:

a. advocate and practice the safe, legal, and responsible use of information and technology

b. exhibit a positive attitude toward using technology that supports collaboration, learning, and productivity

c. demonstrate personal responsibility for lifelong learning

d. exhibit leadership for digital citizenship

6. Technology Operations and Concepts

Students demonstrate a sound understanding of technology concepts, systems, and operations. Students:

a. understand and use technology systems

b. select and use applications effectively and productively

c. troubleshoot systems and applications

d. transfer current knowledge to the learning of new technologies

Index

A

activism by students
   science activism project lesson plan, 145–147
   social activism, tools for, 124–125
   tools for, 81
activity centers as cell phone station, 190
advertising
   cell phone concerns, 15–16
   tools for, 123
alarms on phones, 173
Amber Alerts, 22
Apple
   iCal, 207
   iPhone, 193
art
   art galleries, 124
   Myartspace, 209
artists, messages about, 125
assessment of students, 35–36
assistive technology, 198–199
athletic events, 194–195
AT&T
   mobile storage, 196
   Smart Limits, 199
Audacity
   math ringtone rap or jingle lesson plan, 127
   mobile business campaigns, 123
   physics sound waves lesson plan, 67, 69–70
   ringtones, 112–113
audio editing, future of, 194–195
audio scavenger hunt lesson plan, 109
Audioblogger (now Gabcast), 38, 39f
audioTagger, 24

B

blip.tv
   about, 72, 76, 77t
   mobile television, student-run, 80
   news broadcasts, 79
   student activism, 81

Blogger
   about, 72–73, 77t
   data collection, 78
   local landmarks photoblog lesson plan,
      83–85
   mobile homework help blog lesson plan, 151
   oral history project lesson plan, 40–42, 45
   poetry slam podcast lesson plan, 53
blogs
   mobile, 118–119
   mobile homework help blog lesson plan,
      151–153
BlogTalkRadio (CINCH), 202
BooksInMyPhone, 193
bottom-up approach to technology in schools,
   9–10
BrainCast, 204
brainstorming
   tools for, 35
   Wiffiti, 114–115, 115f
business campaigns, mobile, 123

C

calculators on cell phones, 174
calendars on cell phones, 173
camcorders, cell phones as. *See also* blip.tv; cell
   phone cameras and camcorders; Eyespot;
   YouTube
   blip.tv, 72, 76, 77t
   effect on education, 75–76
   Eyespot, 72, 76–77, 77t
   Web 2.0 resources, 206
   YouTube, 72, 76, 77t
cameras, cell phones as. *See also* Blogger; cell
   phone cameras and camcorders; Flagr;
   Flickr; Photobucket
   Blogger, 72–73, 77t
   Flagr, 74–75, 77t
   Flickr, 74, 77t
   Photobucket, 73–74, 77t
   Web 2.0 resources, 206

cell phone cameras and camcorders, 71–110
  cell phones as camcorders, resources for, 75–77, 77t
  cell phones as cameras, resources for, 72–75, 77t
  classroom uses for, 77–81
  lesson plans
    geo-insects, 98–102
    geometry digital storybook, 86–90
    local landmarks photoblog, 83–85
    photomapping, 94–97
    rock identification, 91–93
    scavenger hunts, 108–110
    suggestions for use, 81–82
    telenovela, 103–107
cell phone plans
  discussion of with children, 187f
  starter phones, 199
  student awareness of financial considerations, 15
cell phone podcasting, voice mail, conferencing, and mobile notes, 23–70
  classroom uses, 32–37
  conferencing, 29–30, 31t
  lesson plans
    oral history project, 40–48
    oral quiz, 54–62
    physics sound waves, 67–70
    poetry slam podcast, 49–53
    suggestions for use, 39
    virtual science symposium, 63–66
  mobile notes, 30–31, 31t
  podcasting, 25–27, 31t
  teachers who podcast, 37–38, 37f, 38f, 39f
  using for, 23–25
  voice mail, 28–29, 31t
Cellfish, 207
CellFlix
  CellFlix Festival, 75
  documentaries, 78
Children's Internet Protection Act of 2001, 7
Chord Maestro, 209
CINCH (BlogTalkRadio), 202
citizen journalism, mobile, 179
class/group activities, tools for, 122, 176–177

classroom control of cell phones, 13
classroom projects for cell phones, developing, 111–167
  classroom ideas, 121–126
  lesson plans
    elections, 164–167
    inquiry question ice breaker, 137–139
    math ringtone raps or jingles, 127–130
    mobile homework help blog, 151–153
    Revolutionary War enhanced podcast, 158–163
    science activism project, 145–147
    scientific survey, 154–157
    Stay Healthy!, 148–150
    suggestions for use, 126
    think-alouds, 140–144
    travel postcards, 131–133
    Who Am I?, 134–136
  mobile blogs, 118–119
  mobile presentations and enhanced podcasts, 120
  mobile surveys and polls, 119
  mobile Web sites, 118
  parental involvement, 126
  ringtones, 112–113
  student involvement, 111–112
  text messaging, 114–117, 115f, 116f
  wallpaper and logos, 113
classroom reviews, tools for, 121
classroom Web sites, 171–172
clay animation, 79
closed captioning on cell phones, 198
collaboration, standards for, 216
collages, 124
Columbine High School, 22, 178
communication, standards for, 216
concerns with cell phones in the classroom, 11–22
  advertising, 15–16
  cell phone etiquette, 13–14
  cell phones in school, 12
  classroom control, 13
  financial considerations, 15
  security, 21–22
  student access, 14–15

types of concerns, 11–12
Web publishing, 16–21, 19–20f
conferencing. *See also* FreeConferencePro
    Gabcast, 26
    TalkShoe, 203
    virtual videoconferencing using cell phones,
        198
content-based mobile Web sites, 126
costs
    cell phone plans, 15, 187f, 199
    Hipcast, 27
    Reactee, 145
    Web 2.0 sites, 15
creativity, standards for, 216
critical thinking, standards for, 217
cultural capital, digital technology literacy
    as, 5
culture of students, bringing to the classroom,
    4–5
current events, tools for, 124–125

D
data collection
    Blogger and Flickr, 78
    Jott, 36
    school policies regarding cell phones, 12
debates, tools for, 33
decision making, standards for, 217
digital audio-narrated storybooks, 78
digital citizenship, standards for, 217
digital culture and classroom learning, 5–6
digital image storybooks, 79
digital projectors, cell phones as, 195–196
digital technology literacy, 5
documentaries, tools for, 78
dotMobi addresses, 171

E
e-commerce using cell phones, 197
e-mail
    Jott, 30
    web 2.0 resources, 205
    Web site access, 171
editing features
    audio and video, 194–195

Photobucket, 73
playlists, 27
Edublogs, 151
educational resources, classroom Web sites as,
    171–172
educational software, 192
election lesson plan, 164–167
Elf, 172
emergency situations
    cell phones in schools, 22
    student safety, 178–179
English as a second language (ESL) students,
    31, 37
enhanced podcasts, 120
ESL (English as a second language) students,
    31, 37
etiquette for cell phones
    cell phones as learning tools, 8–9
    concerns with cell phones in the classroom,
        13–14
    preschool and lower elementary school, 186,
        187–188f
    student permission and agreement for cell
        phone usage, 21
Evoca, 202
Excel, 154, 156–157
extracurricular events, managing, 177–178
Eyespot
    about, 72, 76–77, 77t
    classroom activity centers, 190
    clay animation, 79
    documentaries, 78
    election lesson plan, 167
    news broadcasts, 79
    public service announcements, 80
    student activism, 81
    telenovela lesson plan, 103–107
    video scavenger hunt lesson plan, 109–110

F
faxes, cell phones as, 196
FeedM8
    mobile blogs, 118–119
    mobile homework help blog lesson plan,
        151–153

field trips
  tools for managing, 33, 122, 177–178
  younger children, 189
filters for Web 2.0 sites, 6–8
financial considerations. *See* costs
Flagr
  about, 72, 74–75, 77t
  geo-insects lesson plan, 98–102
  geotagging, 81
flashcards, tools for, 121
Flickr
  about, 72, 74, 77t
  data collection, 78
  digital image storybooks, 79
  field trips with younger children, 189
  geotagging, 80–81
  homework assignments using cell phones,
    190
  image scavenger hunt lesson plan, 108
  mobile citizen journalism, 179
  photomapping lesson plan, 94–97
  rock identification lesson plan, 91–93
  Wiffiti background images, 115
Flixwagon, 76
Flurry, 205
foreign languages
  ESL students, 31, 37
  FeedM8, 118–119
FreeConferencePro
  brainstorming, 35
  conference calls, 25
  conferencing, 29–30, 31t
  conferencing feature, 26
  debates, 33
  guest speakers, virtual, 34–35
  homework tools for managing, 182–183
  interviews, 33
  parents, connecting with, 182
  struggling students, 181
  student absenteeism, 180
  student supervision, 176
  teacher absenteeism, 181
  virtual science symposium lesson plan,
    63–66
Frucall, 208

future of cell phones in schools, 191–200
  assistive technology, 198–199
  digital projectors, 195–196
  e-commerce, 197
  educational software, 192
  faxes and scanners, 196
  features on phones, increase of, 191–192
  GPS tools and tracking, 195
  live streaming, audio editing, and video
    editing, 194–195
  M-government, 199–200
  mobile storage, 196
  MP3 players, recorders, and radios, 193
  point and click, 198
  solar-powered cell phones, 200
  starter phones and phone plans, 199
  writing, literature, and textbooks, 192–193

G
Gabcast
  about, 25–26, 31t
  audio posts to the Internet, 24
  audio scavenger hunt lesson plan, 109
  brainstorming, 35
  election lesson plan, 166
  example of, 38, 38f
  field trips with younger children, 189
  group activities, 176–177
  interviews, 32, 33
  landlines for students without cell phones, 14
  mobile business campaigns, 123
  oral history project lesson plan, 40, 43–48
  original work, 34
  parents, connecting with, 182
  public speaking, 33
  radio broadcasts, 32
  struggling students, 181
  students with special needs, 36–37
Gaggle
  Gabcast accounts, 43
  Jott accounts, 67, 68
GarageBand
  math ringtone rap or jingle lesson plan, 127
  mobile business campaigns, 123

Gcast
    about, 26–27, 31t
    audio posts to the Internet, 24
    example of, 37–38, 37f
    field trips with younger children, 189
    interviews, 32, 33
    landlines for students without cell phones, 14
    original work, 34
    poetry slam podcast lesson plan, 49–53
    public speaking, 33
    radio broadcasts, 32
geometry digital storybook lesson plan, 86–90
geotagging, tools for, 80–81
global positioning systems (GPS) in cell
    phones, 195
Gmail, 171
Google Calendar, 207
Google Mobile, 205
Google Web site access, 171
GoogleEarth, 102
GPS (global positioning systems) in cell
    phones, 195
graphing calculators, 174
group/class activities, tools for, 122, 176–177
groups for messages
    Pinger, 204
    YouMail, 29
guest speakers, virtual, 34–35

H
health education, 209–210
hearing difficulties, assistive technology for,
    198
Hipcast
    about, 27, 31t
    audio posts to the Internet, 24
    field trips with younger children, 189
    interviews, 32, 33
    original work, 34
    public speaking, 33
    radio broadcasts, 32
homework
    assignments using cell phones, 189–190
    mobile homework help blog lesson plan,
        151–153

tools for managing, 182–183
    Twitter, 116–117
    YouMail, 28–29
HomeworkNOW, 171–172
hotlines, cell phone access to, 179

I
I Want Sandy, 207
image scavenger hunt lesson plan, 108
iMovie, 79
information fluency, standards for, 217
innovation, standards for, 216
inquiry question ice breaker lesson plan,
    137–139
Institute for Alternatives in Education, 192
interviews, tools for, 32–33
iPhone
    mobile storage, 196
    MP3 player, 193
iPods, 163
IQzone, 197
iSight, 198

J
Jangl, 203
Jott
    brainstorming, 35
    data collection, 36
    field trips, 33, 178
    field trips with younger children, 189
    local landmarks photoblog lesson plan, 85
    mobile notes, 25, 30–31, 31t
    Nozbe, coupled with, 206–207
    parents, connecting with, 182
    physics sound waves lesson plan, 67–70
    Remember The Milk, coupled with, 207
    students with special needs, 37
Jott Links, 30–31
Jumpcut, 93

K
KidPix, 190
kinesthetic disabilities, students with, 36
KWL technique, tools for, 122

L

landlines
  BrainCast, 204
  Gabcast, 26
  Gcast, 53
  student access to cell phones, 14
Last Spotted, 206
LeapFrog, 199
learning tools, cell phones as, 3–10
  benefits of, 3
  bottom-up approach to technology in
    schools, 9–10
  digital culture, connecting to classroom
    learning, 5–6
  digital etiquette, 8–9
  student culture, bringing to the classroom,
    4–5
  Web 2.0 generation and filters, 6–8
Lee, Deborah, 38, 39f
libraries with text-messaging services, 172
literacies
  digital, 5
  multiple, 4–5
  text messaging as, 116–117
literacy theory approach to learning, 4–5
literature and cell phone use, 192–193
live streaming with cell phones, 194–195
LiveJournal, 151
local landmarks photoblog lesson plan, 83–85
logos
  resources for, 207
  tools for, 113

M

M-generation, adolescents as, 5
M-government using cell phones, 199–200
management tools, cell phones as, 175–183
  field trips and extracurricular events,
    177–178
  group activities, 176–177
  homework help, 182–183
  mobile citizen journalism, 179
  parents, connecting with, 182
  struggling students, 181
  student absenteeism, 180

student safety, 178–179
student supervision, 176
teacher absenteeism, 180–181
map-posting, 74–75
math ringtone rap or jingle lesson plan,
  127–130
mathematics, tools for, 124
Math4Mobile, 192
mob5, 172
.mobi addresses, 171
Mobilatory, 158, 162, 207
Mobile Generation Report, 200
mobile homework help blog lesson plan,
  151–153
MobileQuery, 206
MobiOde
  mathematics, 124
  mobile surveys and polls, 119
  scientific survey lesson plan, 154–157
MobiTV, 193, 194
Moje, Elizabeth, 4
MoneyManager, 192
Movie Maker, 79
movie serials, tools for, 123
MP3 players, 193
multiple literacy approach to learning, 4–5
multiple unique voice-mail greetings, 28
multitasking, 5
Murmur project, 24
music, tools for, 209
Myartspace, 209
MyBuddyQuiz, 208
myFoodPhone, 210
MySpace, 166

N

National Educational Technology Standards
  for Students (NETS•S)
  concerns with cell phones in the classroom,
    17, 18, 19
  standards listed, 216–218
navigation systems in cell phones, 195
NETS•S. *See* National Educational
  Technology Standards for Students
  (NETS•S)

news broadcasts, tools for, 79
Nokia
   e-commerce using cell phones, 197
   Point&Find technology, 198
   radios in phones, 193
nonprofit organizations
   science activism project lesson plan, 147
   tools for, 124–125
notepad features on cell phones, 173–174
notes
   Jott, 30–31, 31t
   Web 2.0 resources, 204
   Wiffiti, 115–116
Nozbe, 207
NTT DoCoMo, 200
Nuance Talks, 198
Nuance Zooms, 198

O

Obama, Barack, 116f, 117
observations, tool for, 115
opportunity for future assignments,
   discussing with students, 21
oral history project lesson plan, 40–48
oral quiz lesson plan, 54–62
organizational tools, 206–207. *See also*
   research and organizational tools, cell
   phones as
original work, tools for, 34

P

parents
   cell phone ownership by younger children,
   186
   classroom projects, involvement in, 126
   connecting with, 182
   homework assignments using cell phones,
   189–190
   volunteers, monitoring, 177
PDAs (personal digital assistants), 173
People's 311, 179
permission forms
   student agreement, 21
   Web publishing, 17–18, 19–20f
personal digital assistants (PDAs), 173

Pew Internet & American Life Project "How
   Americans Use Their Cell Phones," 8
Phixir, 74
Phonezoo
   election lesson plan, 164, 165
   math ringtone rap or jingle lesson plan,
   127–130
   parental involvement in classroom projects,
   126
   poetry, publishing, 121
   ringtone classroom reviews, 121
   ringtones, 112–113
   travel postcard lesson plan, 133
Photobucket
   about, 72, 73–74, 77t
   digital audio-narrated storybooks, 78
   geometry digital storybook lesson plan,
   86–90
   news broadcasts, 79
photomapping lesson plan, 94–97
physics sound waves lesson plan, 67–70
Pilotfish, 198
Pinger, 204
PixDrop, 207
Pix2Fone
   election lesson plan, 164, 165
   field trips and class activities, 122
   math ringtone rap or jingle lesson plan, 130
   mobile business campaigns, 123
   parental involvement in classroom projects,
   126
   sending projects home using cell phones,
   190
   tools for, 123
   travel postcard lesson plan, 131–133
   wallpaper and logos, 113
playlists
   Gcast editing feature, 27
   Hipcast, 27
Plusmo, 172
Pocket Films Festival, 75
podcast, defined, 23
podcasting
   Gabcast, 25–26, 31t
   Gcast, 26–27, 31t

Hipcast, 27, 31t
Web 2.0 resources for cell phones, 202
poetry
    poetry slam podcast lesson plan, 49–53
    publishing, tools for, 121
point and click information retrieval, 198
Point&Find technology, 198
politicians
    messages about, 125
    Twitter, 116–117, 116f
Poll Everywhere
    current events, 124–125
    election lesson plan, 164, 165–166
    field trips, 122
    KWL technique, 122–123
    mathematics, 124
    mobile surveys and polls, 119–120
    scientific survey lesson plan, 157
PowerPoint
    mobile presentations and enhanced
        podcasts, 120
    Revolutionary War enhanced podcast lesson
        plan, 158–160
predators on Web 2.0 sites, 7
preschool and lower elementary school, cell
    phones in, 185–190
    cell phone etiquette, 186, 187–188f
    one cell phone inside the classroom, 190
    one cell phone outside the classroom,
        189–190
    ownership by younger children, 185–186
    student ownership, 189
presentations, mobile, 120
privacy
    Gabcast, 26
    Gcast, 27
    Photobucket, 73
    Web publishing, 16–17
    YouMail, 29
problem solving, standards for, 217
projects, sending home using cell phones, 190
public podcast channels, 26
public service announcements, 80
public speaking, tools for, 33

Q
Qik, 76
Qipit
    fax, copy, and scan capability, 196
    student absenteeism, 180
QuickTimePro, 158, 160–161, 163
quizzes
    mobile, 208
    oral quiz lesson plan, 54–62

R
Radar, 206
radio-frequency identification (RFID) tags,
    197
radios
    future of cell phones in schools, 193
    podcasting, 32
    radio serials, tools for, 123
Rave, 179
Reactee
    artists, academics, and politicians, 125
    current events, 124–125
    election lesson plan, 164–165, 166
    mobile business campaigns, 123
    school events, 125
    science activism project lesson plan,
        145–147
    social activism, 124–125
    text messaging, 117
read/write Web, 6
"Ready to Learn Cell Phone Study," 186
ready.mobi, 171
really simple syndication (RSS)
    audio posts to the Internet, 24
    Flurry, 205
recorders, cell phones as, 193
reference tools, 206
Remember The Milk, 207
research, standards for, 217
research and organizational tools, cell phones
    as, 169–174
    calculators, 175
    calendars, voice recorders, and notepads,
        173–174

classroom Web sites and educational resources, 171–172
convenience of, 169
libraries with text-messaging services, 172
Web site access, 171
Web surfing, benefits of, 170–171
responsibility, discussing with students, 21
Revolutionary War enhanced podcast lesson plan, 158–163
RFID (radio-frequency identification) tags, 197
ringtones
  resources for, 207
  tools for, 112–113
Ripple9, 209
rock identification lesson plan, 91–93
role-playing, tools for, 34
RSS. See really simple syndication (RSS)
rules for cell phone usage by younger children, 187–188f

S
safety and security
  cell phone concerns, 16, 21–22
  field trips, 177
  predators on Web 2.0 sites, 7
  student permission and agreement for cell phone usage, 21
  tools for managing, 178–179
Samsung, 196
Sattler, Pat, 37–38, 37f
scanners, cell phones as, 196
scanR, 196
scavenger hunt lesson plans, 108–110
school administration permission for Web publishing, 17
school events, promoting, 125
school policies regarding cell phones, 11, 12
science activism project lesson plan, 145–147
science jingles and raps, 122
scientific survey lesson plan, 154–157
searchable transcripts of podcasts, 202
shopping
  e-commerce using cell phones, 197
  Frucall, 208

SingTel, 194
skits, tools for, 34
Slippery Rock University, 197
Smart Limits, 199
social activism, tools for, 125
social contracts with students about cell phone use, 13
social-networking sites, 6
social studies jingles and raps, 122
social toys, distractions of, 5–6
solar-powered cell phones, 200
Southeastern Louisiana University, 172
Sparkes, Mary, 38, 38f
speech-to-text e-mails, 30
Sprint, 193
starter phones, 199
Stay Healthy! lesson plan, 148–150
storage on cell phones, 196
student ownership of cell phones, 189
student permission and agreement for cell phone usage, 21
students
  absenteeism, managing, 180
  access to cell phones, 14–15
  keeping track of on field trips, 33
  special needs, with, 36–37
  struggling, tools for, 181
  supervision of, tools for, 176
study groups, 116–117
surveillance systems for cell phones, 194
surveys and polls, mobile, 119. See also Poll Everywhere
Synaptics, 198

T
TalkShoe, 203
teachers
  absenteeism, 180–181
  podcasts by, 37–38, 37f, 38f, 39f
TeacherTube, 107
technology
  bottom-up approach, 9–10
  operations and concepts, standards for, 218
telenovela lesson plan, 103–107
television

MobiTV, 193, 194
student-run, tools for, 80
text messaging
  homework tools for managing, 183
  libraries with text-messaging services, 172
  Reactee, 117
  TextForFree, 114
  Twitter, 116–117, 116f
  Web 2.0 resources for, 208
  Wiffiti, 114–116, 115f
textbooks, future of, 192–193
TextForFree
  current events, 124–125
  election lesson plan, 164, 165
  flashcards, 121–122
  mobile business campaigns, 123
  poetry, publishing, 121
  text messaging, 114
  Who Am I? lesson plan, 134–135
think-aloud lesson plan, 140–144
"To Be Part of the Story: The Literacy
  Practices of Gangsta Adolescents" (Moje), 4
touchpads for assistive technology, 198
tracking capabilities in cell phones, 195
travel postcard lesson plan, 131–133
Twitter
  text messaging, 116–117, 116f
  think-aloud lesson plan, 140–144
Txt2day, 208
txtDrop, 208

U
University of Haifa, 192
UnWired Buyer, 197
Utterz, 202

V
video blogs, 27
video editing, 194–195
video scavenger hunt lesson plan, 109–110
"video share," 194
Virginia Tech, 178
virtual science symposium lesson plan, 63–66
virtual videoconferencing using cell phones,
  198

visual impairment
  assistive technology, 198–199
  Jott, 30
  tools for, 36–37
voice mail
  Jangl, 203
  YouMail, 28–29, 31t
voice messages, 204
voice recorders, 173–174

W
wallpaper
  resources for, 207
  tools for, 113
Wapedia, 171
Wattpad, 193
Wayfinder, 195
Web 2.0 generation, 6–8
Web 2.0 resources for cell phones, 201–210
  camera and camcorder resources, 206
  conferencing, 203
  health education, 209–210
  logos, wallpaper, and ringtones, 207
  mobile notes, 204
  mobile quizzes, 208
  mobile shopping, 208
  mobile Web sites, 205
  music and art, 209
  podcasting, 202
  reference and organizational tools, 206–207
  RSS, e-mail, and favorites, 205
  text messaging, 208
  voice mail, 203
Web publishing, 16–21, 19–20f
Web sites, mobile
  access to, with cell phones, 171
  school policies regarding cell phones, 12
  tools for, 118
  Winksite, 205
Web surfing benefits with cell phones,
  170–171
Who Am I? lesson plan, 134–136
Wiffiti
  field trips, 122

inquiry question ice breaker lesson plan, 137–139

KWL technique, 122–123

text messaging, 114–116, 115f

Wikipedia, 171

Winksite, 205

Wood, Joe, 115, 115f

writing using cell phones, 192–193

Y

Yahoo, 171

Yahoo Mobile, 205

YouMail

  assessment of students, 35–36

  brainstorming, 35

  field trips, 177

  oral quiz lesson plan, 54–62

teacher absenteeism, 180–181

voice mail, 24–25, 28–29, 31t

YouTube

  about, 72, 76, 77t

  mobile television, student-run, 80

  news broadcasts, 79

  student activism, 81

Z

Zinadoo

  classroom reviews, 121-122

  content-based mobile Web sites, 126

  election lesson plan, 164, 165

  mobile business campaigns, 123

  mobile Web sites, 118

  school events, 125–126

  Stay Healthy! lesson plan, 148–150

Credits

Cover
Artwork: © 2008 Jupiterimages Corporation

Chapter 2
pg. 11: image © 2008 Jupiterimages
Corporation

Chapter 3
pg. 23 image:
© istockphoto.com/Galina Barskaya
Audacity screenshots: © 2008 members
of the Audacity development team
Blogger screenshots: © Google
Deborah Lee's Podcast used with permission
FreeConferencePro screenshots:
© FreeConferencePro
Gabcast screenshots:
© Coalescent Systems, Inc.
Gcast screenshots: © GarageBand Records
Jott screenshots: © Jott Networks Inc.
Mary Sparkes's Lit. & Tech Podcast used with
permission
Patt Sattler's St. Joe's Podcast used with
permission
YouMail screenshots: © YouMail, Inc.

Chapter 4
pg. 71 image:
© 2008 Jupiterimages Corporation
Blogger screenshots: © Google
Eyespot screenshots: © Eyespot Corporation
Flagr screenshots: © Flagr Inc.
Flickr screenshots: © Yahoo! Inc.
FreeConferencePro screenshots:
© FreeConferencePro
Gabcast screenshots:
© Coalescent Systems, Inc.
Photobucket screenshots: © Photobucket Inc.

Chapter 5
pg. 111 image:
© istockphoto.com/Dmitry Goygel-Sokol
FEEDM8 screenshots: © FEEDM8
Mobilatory screenshots: © Mobilatory.com
MobiOde screenshots:
© Mobile Websites by Wirenode
Phonezoo screenshots:
© Phonezoo Communications, Inc.
Pix2Fone screenshots: www.pix2fone.com
Poll Everywhere screenshots:
© Poll Everywhere, Inc
Powerpoint screenshots:
© Microsoft Corporation
QuickTime Pro screenshots: © Apple Inc.
Reactee screenshots: © Reactee
TextForFree screenshots: © TextForFree.net
Twitter screenshots: © Twitter
Wiffiti screenshots: © LocaModa Inc.
Zinadoo screenshots: © Zinadoo

Chapter 6
pg. 169 image:
© istockphoto.com/Dmitry Nikolaev

Chapter 7
pg. 175 image:
© 2008 Jupiterimages Corporation

Chapter 8
pg. 185 image:
© 2008 Jupiterimages Corporation

Chapter 9
pg. 191 image:
© 2008 Jupiterimages Corporation

Chapter 10
pg. 201: image
© istockphoto.com/Luis Pedrosa